Abbas Kiarostami

Contemporary Film Directors

Edited by James Naremore

The Contemporary Film Directors series provides concise, well-written introductions to directors from around the world and from every level of the film industry. Its chief aims are to broaden our awareness of important artists, to give serious critical attention to their work, and to illustrate the variety and vitality of contemporary cinema. Contributors to the series include an array of internationally respected critics and academics. Each volume contains an incisive critical commentary, an informative interview with the director, and a detailed filmography.

A list of books in the series appears at the end of this book.

Abbas Kiarostami

Mehrnaz Saeed-Vafa
and
Jonathan Rosenbaum

UNIVERSITY
OF
ILLINOIS
PRESS
URBANA
AND
CHICAGO

Manufactured in the United States of America
1 2 3 4 5 C P 7 6 5 4 3

This book is printed on acid-free paper.

Library of Congress Cataloging-in-Publication Data
Saeed-Vafa, Mehrnaz, 1950–
Abbas Kiarostami / Mehrnaz Saeed-Vafa and Jonathan Rosenbaum.
p. cm. — (Contemporary film directors)
Includes bibliographical references and index.
ISBN 978-0-252-02814-4 (cloth: alk. paper)
ISBN 978-0-252-07111-9 (pbk. : alk. paper)
1. Kiarostami, Abbas—Criticism and interpretation.
I. Rosenbaum, Jonathan. II. Title. III. Series.
PN1998.3.K58S23 2003
791.43'0233'092—dc21 2002011214

Frontispiece: Abbas Kiarostami at the Locarno International
Film Festival, August 1995

Contents

Preface and Acknowledgments

The theory behind this book's methodology isn't only that two heads are better than one but also that two viewpoints from different cameras—especially if they came from separate cultures and could interact and communicate with each other—might bring greater depth to a study of Abbas Kiarostami. The two essays that begin this book were written simultaneously and developed concurrently—both cover the body of Abbas Kiarostami's work, but from somewhat different angles and with the benefit of separate contexts. In the following dialogue, the authors seek to clarify those angles and contexts as well as discuss various points of disagreement and convergence. Finally, their interviews with Kiarostami, conducted between 1998 and 2001, will hopefully illuminate and broaden some of the issues raised.

For diverse kinds of assistance, the authors would like to thank Jamsheed Akrami, Brian Andriotti, Mohammed Atebbai, Michael Beard, Mahmud Behraznia, Godfrey Cheshire, Amir Esfandiari, Jean-Michel Frodon, John Gianvito, Houshang Golmakini, Kent Jones, Mahoud Kalari, Ahmad Karimi-Hakkak, Hossein Khandan, Frank Lewis, Patrick Z. McGavin, Mitra Mohaseni, James Naremore, Mahvash Sheikh Ol-Islami, Mohammad Pakshir, Ray Privett, Aziz Saati, Seifollah Samadian, Martin Scorsese, and, in particular, Abbas Kiarostami.

Abbas Kiarostami

Abbas Kiarostami

Jonathan Rosenbaum

I want to give the audience a hint of a scene. No more than that. Give them too much and they won't contribute anything themselves. Give them just a suggestion and you get them working with you. That's what gives the theatre meaning: when it becomes a social act.

—Orson Welles, 1938

It's an unavoidable truism that any effort to nail down the specifics of a national cinematic "new wave" in an authoritative manner is doomed to a certain amount of mythmaking. Regarding the French New Wave, the term sprang from casual journalism in the 1950s and generally wound up meaning among journalists whatever they wanted it to mean: dozens of first-time French directors who either got bankrolled, made a splash, or both over the same period (the most common definition); habitués of the Paris Cinémathèque who became filmmakers; young *Cahiers du cinéma* critics who went from theory to practice; a thematically (or romantically) oriented youth movement; and so on.

The Iranian New Wave, then, is not one but many potential movements, each with a somewhat different time frame and honor roll. Although I first heard this term in the early 1990s, I only began recognizing the Iranian New Wave as a genuine movement—that is, a discernible tendency in terms of social and political concerns, poetics, and overall quality—toward the end of that decade. Some, including Mehrnaz Saeed-Vafa, have plausibly cited Sohrab Shahid Saless's *A Simple Event* (1973—a film Kiarostami has cited as a major influence) as a seminal work.[1] Another key founding gesture, pointing to a quite different definition and history, is Kiarostami's own *Close-up* (1990).[2]

I'd like to propose a lesser-known short film preceding both of these and contemporary with the French New Wave: Forugh Farrokhzad's *The House Is Black* (1962), a twenty-two-minute documentary about a leper colony outside Tabriz. For the filmmaker Mohsen Makhmalbaf, it is "the best Iranian film [to have] affected the contemporary Iranian cinema," despite (or maybe because) of the fact that Forugh "never went to a college to study cinema".[3] It is also, to the best of my knowledge, the first Iranian documentary made by a woman. It was seen in the West and clearly made an impression, winning a prize at the Oberhausen Film Festival in 1963 and also showing at the Pesaro Film Festival in 1966. For me, among the sixty or seventy I've seen to date, it's the greatest of all Iranian films. I hope readers will forgive my focusing here on a film not easy to see (though there are indications that it may be out soon on DVD); for me its importance as well as its pertinence to Kiarostami warrant such a treatment (although I hasten to add that if this book was about Makhmalbaf, *The House Is Black* would be just as relevant).

More than any other Iranian film that comes to mind, *The House Is Black* highlights the paradox that while Iranians continue to be among the most demonized people on the planet (along with their neighbors to the west, the Iraqis), Iranian cinema is becoming almost universally recognized by critics as among the most ethical and humanist. Confused fears are still often allowed to dictate impressions of a country of almost 65 million individuals—more people than can be found in either France or the United Kingdom, comprising a population whose melting-pot diversity might actually be said to resemble that of the United States. Moreover, 65 percent of the country is currently under the age of 25 (and the age at which Iranians can vote is much younger than in the United States, which confounds most stereotypes even further).

Why, one may ask, has there been this demonization? Two major factors appear to be at play. The most obvious one is the Iranian hostage crisis during the Carter administration (November 1979–January

1981), which appears to have congealed most Western images of Iranians into a single one of fanatical, fundamentalist terrorists. (Prior to this event, a CIA-orchestrated coup in 1953 ousted Prime Minister Mohammed Mossadegh to install the friendly shah and break the nationalist movement. This move, unacknowledged in the United States for well over forty years, played a significant part in Iran in demonizing the role of American influence.) The second major factor is that practically no other contemporary image of Iran has been available in the West to counter or even complicate the fundamentalist stereotype.

It might be argued, indeed, that the emergence of the Iranian New Wave on the international film scene was motivated in part by a desire to fill in a blank page. Yet many Iranians would complain that the new images thrown up by Iranian cinema were stereotypes about salt-of-the-earth peasants—more benign than the preceding stereotypes, to be sure, but still essentially misleading. In this respect, the images of poor lepers in *The House Is Black,* which can't even pretend to be typical or characteristic, offer a bracing alternative.

Farrokhzad (1935–67)—widely regarded as the greatest Iranian woman poet and the greatest twentieth-century Iranian poet, who died in a car accident at thirty-two—made *The House Is Black* at twenty-seven, working over twelve days with a small crew. The following year, in an interview, she "expressed deep personal satisfaction with the project insofar as she had been able to gain the lepers' trust and become their friend while among them."[4] I mainly want to consider the film here not so much for its possible influence on Kiarostami, which is difficult to establish in any case (despite the fact that when I saw the film for the first time, without subtitles, at the Locarno Film Festival in 1995, during the first major Kiarostami retrospective, he was seated a few rows behind me), as for its importance as a founding gesture of the Iranian New Wave. On a more personal level, Saeed-Vafa and I worked with three others in subtitling *The House Is Black* in English prior to its screening at the New York Film Festival in 1997, on the same program as Kiarostami's *Taste of Cherry* (1997). Though it was dismissed in a single sentence by the *New York Times*'s reviewer, it clearly made a strong impression on many others who saw it there and in subsequent U.S. screenings before the print was returned to the Swiss Cinémathèque,[5] and it has also been seen recently in London.

Defying standard taboos concerning lepers—especially the injunction to avoid physical contact with them for her own safety—Forugh wound up permanently adopting the son of two lepers in the colony, Hosein, taking him with her to Tehran to live at her mother's house. Yet some of the film's first viewers criticized it for exploiting lepers by employing them as metaphors for Iranians under the shah or more generally using them for her own purposes rather than theirs.[6]

When I first heard about the latter charge I was shocked, for much of the film's primal force resides in what I would call its radical humanism, which goes beyond anything I know in Western cinema. It would be fascinating as well as instructive to pair *The House Is Black* with Tod Browning's 1932 fiction feature *Freaks*,which oscillates between empathy and horror for its real-life cast of freaks. By contrast, Farrokhzad's uncanny capacity to regard lepers without morbidity as both beautiful and ordinary, objects of love as well as intense identification, offers very different challenges, pointing to very different spiritual and philosophical assumptions.

At the same time, any attentive reading of *The House Is Black* is obliged to conclude that certain parts of its "documentary realism" (perhaps most obviously, its closing scene in a classroom as well as the powerful cutaway shot of the colony's gates closing that occurs just before the end) must have been staged as well as scripted. Farrokhzad, like later Iranian New Wave filmmakers working with nonprofessionals in relatively impoverished locations, created rather than simply found, conjuring up a potent blend of actuality and fiction that makes the two register as coterminous rather than as dialectical. Much more dialectical is the relationship between the film's two narrators—an unidentified male voice describing leprosy factually and relatively dispassionately, albeit with clear humanist assumptions, and Farrokhzad reciting her own poetry in a beautiful, dirgelike tone, halfway between multidenominational prayer and blues lament.

This poetic mixture is also found throughout Kiarostami's work over a span of more than three decades, and it raises comparable issues about the director's manipulation of and control over his cast members. Yet the films of both Farrokhzad and Kiarostami propose inquiries into the ethics of middle-class artists filming poor people: they are not simply or exclusively demonstrations of this practice. In Kiarostami's case, the films are often critiques of the filmmaker's distance and detachment from his subjects as well as his special entitlements, as seen in his work since the early 1980s (both *Orderly or Disorderly* [1981] and *Fellow Citizen* [1983], for instance, feature his offscreen voice). In Farrokhzad's case, in which the sense of personal commitment runs even deeper, the implications of an artist being unworthy of her subject are never entirely absent.

The most obvious parallel to *The House Is Black* in Kiarostami's career is his documentary *A.B.C. Africa* (2001) about orphans of AIDS victims in Uganda. This film goes beyond even Farrokhzad's works in emphasizing the everyday joy of children at play in the midst of their apparent devastation, preferring to show us the victims' pleasure rather than their suffering without in any way minimizing the gravity of their situation. But it's no less important to note that one of Farrokhzad's poems is recited in toto during the most important sequence of Kiarostami's most ambitious feature to date, whose title is the same as the poem's, *The Wind Will Carry Us* (1999).

Even today, in spite of the continuing scandal that she embodies and represents, Farrokhzad is commonly and affectionately referred to by her first name. Her importance in Iranian life and culture points to the special status in Iran of poetry, which might even be said to compete with Islam. *The House Is Black* is to my mind one of the very few successful fusions of literary poetry with film poetry—a blend that commonly invites the worst forms of self-consciousness and pretentiousness—and arguably this linkage of cinema with literature is a fundamental trait underlying much of the Iranian New Wave.

That Farrokhzad was the first woman in Persian literature to write about her sexual desire, and that her own volatile and crisis-ridden life was as central to her legend as her poetry, helps to explain her potency as a political figure who was reviled in the press and placed outside most official literary canons while still being worshipped as both a goddess and a martyr. Despite her enormous differences from the Italian director Pier Paolo Pasolini, it probably wouldn't be too outlandish to see her as a somewhat comparable figure in staging heroic and dangerous shotgun marriages between eros and religion, poetry and politics, poverty and privilege—and as a figure whose violent death has been the focus of comparable mythic speculation. She and her film will remain important throughout this study because of their enormous value as limit cases and artistic models.

| | |

I hasten to add that if Kiarostami for me takes second place to Forugh in relation to Iranian film, I believe he has no competitors at all in contemporary world cinema. Though he remains every bit as controversial wherever his films are shown as French director Jean-Luc Godard was during the 1960s, his influence, which remains enormous, seems mainly concentrated in the Middle East, Iran in particular—a paradox given how widely some of his films are scorned there. As a conduit to Western interest in Iran, he obviously occupies a highly ambiguous position both inside and outside his own culture, stemming as much from what he supposedly represents as from what he does as an artist. From the perspective of some skeptical Iranians, he reinforces stereotypical notions about salt-of-the-earth peasants. Yet from the perspectives of the "incomplete" and "interactive" cinema that he himself proposes, the images of humanity offered, by virtue of being invested with each viewer's imagination, are not singular but plural, varying from one spectator to another, whatever their class orientations. It also seems worth adding that, at least after *Where Is the Friend's House?* (1986), all of Kiarostami's features include wealthy or middle-class characters along with poor ones, and that the films are in fact largely concerned with interactions between poor and well-to-do people.

My own estimation of Kiarostami's art mainly rests on the nearly inexhaustible pleasure I find in his work, and my sense of his importance derives, at least in part, from his capacity to develop in relative independence from the dictates of commercial mainstream cinema. But I can't say that his brilliance was fully apparent to me from the outset; as with the Danish director Carl Dreyer and the French director Jacques Tati, two other favorites, much of my appreciation came in incremental stages. Though I regarded *Life and Nothing More . . .* (1992) as a masterpiece when I first saw it in Locarno in August 1992 and was also immediately impressed by *Close-up*, which I saw a month later, I blush to admit that I initially described *Where Is the Friend's House?* (seen at around the same time as *Close-up*) as "a rather unexceptional cutesy comedy." Not realizing that the title came from a famous Persian poem by Sohrab Sepehry, I even misidentified it as *Where Is My Friend's House?* (an error also made by the film's English and French subtitlers, among others). It was only years later that the film's emotional subtlety and its philosophical and poetic elements began to register. Perhaps in 1992 I was responding adversely to news about the commercial success in Iran of both *Where Is the Friend's House?* and *Close-up* relative to *Life and Nothing More . . .*, a "flop" I much preferred, but this only goes to show how momentary agendas can capriciously affect critical judgments.

But I'm far from being the only slow learner when it comes to appreciating some of the finer points of Kiarostami's art. I find it no less significant that when Kiarostami made *Orderly or Disorderly*—for me the most profound of his short films—he didn't yet regard himself as a film artist (see the interviews in this volume). And for viewers who argue that his status as an "elitist" experimental artist makes him ill-suited for the role of Iran's goodwill ambassador, I can only offer my conviction that only occasionally can the best art equal the best diplomacy—or the best propaganda. (Louis Armstrong, heard at the end of *Taste of Cherry*, may offer the best example.) *Life and Nothing More . . .* describes a semifictional quest that is never resolved within the narrative, in which a film director looks for the lead actors in *Where Is the Friend's House?* after an earthquake has struck the mountainous region where it was shot. This lack of resolution, inaugurating a penchant for narrative ellipsis that continued over Kiarostami's next three features, obviously had a lot to do with the film's relative lack of commercial success. But the presence of these narrative ellipses also clearly refutes the frequent charge that Kiarostami is interested in catering to Western audiences, since many Western viewers are just as annoyed about this lack of narrative closure as Iranians.

For me, the pleasures of an interactive cinema of this kind are predicated on an unalienated view of art that seems rarefied only when one privileges the domestic grosses of blockbusters and willfully ignores the number of people across the planet who clearly enjoy what Kiarostami is doing. Like Godard, Kiarostami can be regarded in part as a child of state funding and his capacity to develop under the protection offered by the bureaucracy of Kanun (the Center for the Intellectual Development of Children and Young Adults, a state organization founded by the shah's wife), away from the usual commercial dictates, is precisely what made viable the play of his early shorts, which were at once childlike and experimental.

| | |

Kiarostami, born in Tehran on June 22, 1940, developed an interest in painting when he was still in grammar school—a time when, according to his own account, he spoke to no one and was a poor student—and the plastic arts dominated his life prior to his involvement in film. In some respects they have dominated his life since then as well: Kiarostami probably devotes as much time today to landscape photography as to film, and the resemblance of these photographs to many of his early landscape paintings is also striking. (The parallels between these two kinds of landscape art seem related to his argument that he sees no clear-cut distinction between documentary and fiction.)

Though he initially flunked out of a university fine arts program after leaving home at eighteen and worked as a traffic cop, he eventually enrolled in another art school and passed, attending classes in the daytime and continuing to direct traffic or working at a desk job in a police office at night. Then he was a commercial artist, designing book covers and posters, and gradually gravitated into TV commercials: he made over 150 between 1960 and 1969, and he designed credit sequences for a good many films over the same period.

Kiarostami was already pushing thirty when Firuz Shirvanlu, the owner of an advertising agency he worked for, a good friend, and the director of Kanun, invited him in 1969 to collaborate in setting up the center's film unit. As Kiarostami put it later, his commercials were regarded as Western in a positive sense by virtue of being slick and stylish, which is presumably why he was the first filmmaker to join the center. He and Shirvanlu spent the better part of a year building soundstages and making other preparations, after which Kiarostami made his first film[7]—a ten-minute comic short in black and white called *Bread and Alley* (1970) about a little boy trying to walk home past an unfriendly dog. The uncredited musical accompaniment—a cheerful jazz version of "Ob-La-Di, Ob-La-Da," a tune on the Beatles' White Album, by either Paul Desmond or someone who sounds very much like him—sets the mood precisely.

Assigned to make educational films in his new post, Kiarostami wound up founding a school of filmmaking in more ways than one, since Kanun went on to produce works by such New Wave filmmakers as

Bahram Beyzae and Amir Naderi. Several other New Wave figures later received part of their training by working as Kiarostami's assistants on feature films, but this influence should be considered apart from the separate, specific influence of Kiarostami's initial project. Over about fifteen years, he sought to create a particular kind of pedagogical cinema, a project that played a substantial role in making films about children fashionable in Iran and also brought a note of playfulness to Iranian filmmaking that had otherwise been struck only rarely (mainly, it seems, in the work of Parviz Kimiavi). Many of these films—*Recess* (1972); *The Traveler* (1974); *Two Solutions for One Problem* (1975); *So Can I* (1975); *Case No. 1, Case No. 2* (1979); *Orderly or Disorderly; First Graders* (1985); *Where Is the Friend's House?; Homework* (1988)—are set wholly or partially inside schools or classrooms (and the second actually has its credits written in chalk on a blackboard, consciously or unconsciously reprising a device from *The House Is Black*). Practically all of them qualify in one way or another as didactic works, analogous to what Bertolt Brecht called "Lehrstücken," or learning plays.[8] (Whether Kiarostami's Kanun films were meant for children is another matter; the last two that he's made to date, *Close-up* and *Life and Nothing More . . .* , clearly aren't.)

What seems especially pertinent is that for Kiarostami, state and institutional funding removed the usual demands of commercial filmmaking, so that he was able to develop his style free of constraints regarding narrative, action, and subject matter. Using the National Film Board of Canada and the director Norman McLaren as early models (see interviews in this volume for more information), he could reflect on issues of loyalty raised by the Iranian Revolution (in *Case No. 1, Case No. 2*) or the advantages of cooperation over conflict (in *Two Solutions for One Problem*); draw on animation (used briefly in *So Can I*) or abstraction (as in *The Colors* [1976]); raise philosophical questions about order (*Orderly or Disorderly*) or formal as well as social questions about sound (in *The Chorus* (1982)); show why dental hygiene is important (in a short of that name); or compare the behavior and excuses of various drivers trying to get through a blocked intersection (in *Fellow Citizen*). More broadly, he could proceed like an experimental filmmaker (or turn to parable-like narratives in such short features as *The Experience* [1973], *The Wedding Suit* [1976], and *The Traveler*) without being made to feel that he was shirking any of his social duties. On the contrary, one might say that he largely used this Kanun project as a pretext for educating himself and that an ethical self-inquiry has been at the roots of his filmmaking ever since. (*Where Is the Friend's House?* for instance, is essentially a film about how difficult it is to be ethical. This theme is given an ironic inflection by the film's final line: a stern teacher in class says, "Good boy," which reveals how little he actually knows about the matter at hand.)

Two Solutions for One Problem, one of the finest shorts, shows what happens in a classroom after Dara borrows a book from Nader and returns it with its cover torn. The film is like a deadpan, Bressonian restaging of one of Laurel and Hardy's epic grudge matches: Nader tears the cover of Dara's book, Dara breaks Nader's pencil, Nader rips Dara's shirt, Dara breaks Nader's ruler, and so on, in syncopated time. An animated two-column chart on a blackboard chalks up whose objects are destroyed; then the story begins again with Dara gluing back Nader's book cover, the bell ringing for recess, and the boys exiting as friends.

A recurring formal principle of parallelism in these Kanun documentaries anticipates some of the repetitive elements in Kiarostami's later features, such as the successive takes of the film being shot in *Through the Olive Trees* (1994) or the many drives up a hill to speak on a cellular phone in *The Wind Will Carry Us.* Some of these elements are even repeated from one feature to the next, such as the extended and extreme long shots concluding *Life and Nothing More . . .* and *Through the Olive Trees* (1994), which are already anticipated in certain shots toward the end of *Report* (1977). What I have in mind is a certain kind of construction in which a repeated shot, camera setup, narrative situation, or editing pattern structures the film as a whole. Children imitate the movements of other creatures in matching shots in *So Can I;* postrevolutionary authorities of various kinds comment on the same classroom dilemma with two different outcomes in *Case No. 1, Case No. 2;* contrasting forms of behavior, as seen and as filmed, are the subject of *Orderly or Disorderly;* and the drivers in *Fellow Citizen* are usually filmed from the same angle with a telephoto lens, recalling some of the documentary strategies in Tati's *Trafic* (1971).

Used for humorous as well as analytical purposes, with implications that can be poetic as well as sociological, these parallel constructions are the building blocks that eventually evolved into the larger structures of

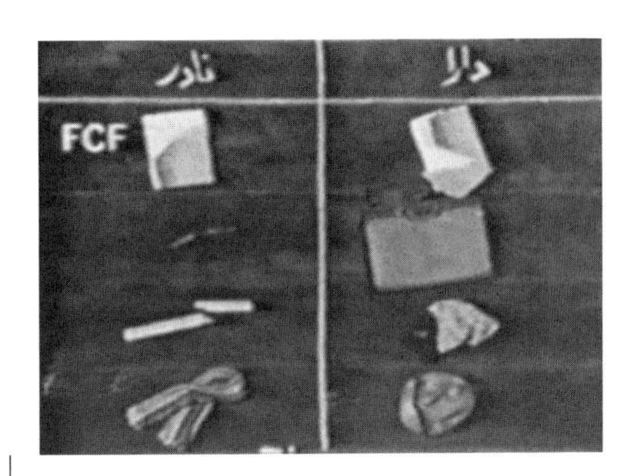

Toting up the final damage in *Two Solutions for One Problem*

the recent features. They are perhaps first of all ways of posing questions, and it should be stressed that Kiarostami belongs to that tribe of filmmakers for whom a shot is often closer to being a question than an answer—a tribe including, among others, John Cassavetes, Otto Preminger, Jacques Rivette, Andrei Tarkovsky, and Tati in his last three features. Significantly, all these filmmakers, with the exception of Cassavetes, have a particular predilection for what might be termed philosophical long shots and all the questions these imply.

If *The Traveler,* Kiarostami's fourth and final black-and-white film to date (after *Bread and Alley, Recess,* and *The Experience*) and first full-length feature, qualifies as his first masterpiece, it's an uncharacteristic one insofar as it relies more heavily on narrative than most of the others. It is also probably closer to Italian neorealism than any of his other films. It does give us a prototypical, tragicomic Kiarostami hero, an earlier version of which was already introduced in *The Experience:* a male character, single-mindedly bent on accomplishing a particular task, whose monomaniacal concentration isolates him from the surrounding community and who ultimately winds up in some sort of failure or impasse. In *The Experience* the hero is a boy working in a photography shop who's smitten with a middle-class girl and hopes to get a job working at her house. In *The Traveler* the ambition—to attend a soccer match in Tehran—is somewhat more ignoble, and the hero winds up missing it only by falling asleep outside the stadium (occasioning the only Kiaro-

A boy with an empty camera in *The Traveler*

stami dream sequence to date, a disturbing nightmare involving guilt as well as persecution that plays largely in silence). The hero has raised his bus fare by pretending to take pictures of schoolmates with his empty camera, which marks the first instance (among many) of media manipulation and exploitation in Kiarostami's work.

Discounting the commissioned documentary *Jahan Nama Palace* (1974), which qualifies as little more than an industrial film, the two odd films out in Kiarostami's first decade of filmmaking are *Report* and *Case No. 1, Case No. 2*. These, made just before and just after the Revolution, are the two films in his oeuvre that have met most directly with state censorship (in the first case, through the suppression of at least two sequences; in the second, through the eventual banning of the film in its entirety; see Saeed-Vafa's account of both films in this volume). *Report*—framed by the parallelism of credits at the beginning and end in the form of an official report being typed out—is Kiarostami's only significant early film made without Kanun's sponsorship, and it might even be regarded as his first effort to make a "commercial" feature. Yet it is also without question his most unpleasant film as well as the only one in which his project of ethical self-inquiry comes up short: it is a provocative yet unsuccessful work informed and no doubt confused by its autobiographical elements. Specifically, its depiction of a disintegrating marriage—made around the same time that Kiarostami's marriage was disintegrating and after both his sons were born—seems to be a mainly unconvincing effort to make this rift register as a reflection of contemporary society. When Kiarostami remarks ambiguously in an interview in this volume, "I was always inside—the camera was inside—so it's totally different [from my other films,]" it's not clear whether he's referring to shooting in interiors or dealing with psychological turmoil, but both meanings seem to apply.

By contrast, *Case No. 1, Case No. 2* owes most of its interest today to its value as a historical record of Iran just after the Revolution, rather than to any personal aspects or to its awkward use of a form of parallel construction that would yield better results in other films. Though it certainly bears Kiarostami's stamp, its main significance is that he happened to be in the right place at the right time to record the postrevolutionary discourse of several individuals, some of whom emigrated or died shortly afterward.

| | |

One can speak of different quantum leaps between Kiarostami's early and later films, but none seems quite as remarkable as the chasm separating *First Graders* and *Homework,* his first two full-length documentary features. Both qualify as investigative journalism set in grammar schools located in working-class neighborhoods, and it would be easy to call the former sixteen-millimeter film a sketch for the latter, except that wouldn't explain why *First Graders* is conventional and relatively uninteresting while *Homework* is subtle, innovative, and masterful. In between these documentaries Kiarostami would make another masterpiece, *Where Is the Friend's House?* which is also about schoolchildren doing homework (and which I'll discuss at length only after I deal with *Close-up,* so that it can be considered alongside the two other Kiarostami features made in the same part of northern Iran). It hardly seems like an exaggeration to assert that Kiarostami forged his artistic identity when he made the latter two features, because important facets of his subsequent work can be traced back to them. To cite only three examples: he acknowledges his own presence as a significant and often determining factor in the proceedings (literally in *Homework, Close-up, Taste of Cherry,* and *A.B.C. Africa;* implicitly in *Life and Nothing More . . . , Through the Olive Trees,* and *The Wind Will Carry Us*); he suppresses a portion of the sound track for ambiguous reasons during the final sequences of both *Homework* and *Close-up;* and he explores the exteriors of an ancient village clinging to the side of a mountain in *Where Is the Friend's House?* and *The Wind Will Carry Us*.

Kiarostami's own presence or lack thereof is certainly one of the major factors separating *First Graders* from *Homework*. The earlier film in fact traffics in the sort of deception criticized in Kiarostami's later work by refusing to acknowledge either the presence of the filmmakers or the powers they enjoy in recording the responses of six-year-old boys sent to the principal's office in a school located in one of the poorest sections of Tehran. Evocative at times of some of Frederick Wiseman's early documentaries, *First Graders* places far too much emphasis on the paternal "wisdom" of the principal dispensing justice, which implicitly valorizes Kiarostami's own position without ever really examining it.

This sort of tainted relationship between filmmaker and subject begins to be acknowledged as well as critiqued in *Homework*, in which Kiarostami films himself interviewing schoolboys of roughly the same age as the boys in *First Graders* about how they do their homework, after introducing himself at the outset as the filmmaker and narrator. "It's not a movie in the usual sense," he says offscreen to another adult as we see several boys on their way to school. "It's research—pictorial research on children's homework." He goes on to explain that he got the idea to do this while helping one of his own sons with his homework, and shortly afterward we see the boys in the schoolyard reciting elaborate Islamic chants while performing calisthenics.

It's a straightforward way of approaching his material. Yet in the very act of cutting to reverse-angle shots of himself and his cameraman during the interviews—shots that obviously (or not-so-obviously, at least to the casual viewer) require the services of an additional cameraman, who isn't being acknowledged—Kiarostami begins to foreground some of the implicit contradictions of his own deceptiveness in the pursuit of documentary truth.

It's only in *Close-up*, his next and decisive encounter with the documentary form, that he takes on the subject of the filmmaker's role directly,making it an integral part of his theme. In *Homework* the foregrounding is more ambiguous. Maybe he's deceiving us in a trivial way by not showing us his second cameraman, who in fact filmed the reverse angles after the interviews as inserts to be intercut later. Yet we also have to admit that if Kiarostami had bothered to show us this second cameraman, this may have only distracted us from matters that are far more important: the children he's filming, the emotions and attitudes that they conceal as well as reveal, and what these tell us about their parents, their school, and their society.

This is essentially why the film critic Gilberto Perez disagreed with an earlier observation of mine about Kiarostami, in which I used the word *lying* instead of *deceptiveness* and argued that Kiarostami in *Homework* and *Close-up* was deconstructing, or unpacking, the documentary form. Perez countered that in *Homework* Kiarostami was "after bigger game than the cheating regularly (or irregularly) practiced in documentaries"—namely the cowering of the children before authorities (including the camera's authority) that ruled their lives at a time when Iran was still at war with Iraq.[9]

I take his point. In the penultimate sequence of *Homework*—after a wrenching interview in which a boy is crying inconsolably and begging to see his friend—the kids are once again reciting religious war chants and beating their chests in the school yard. Kiarostami dryly remarks offscreen that because they're performing this ceremony "incorrectly," he's decided as a gesture of respect to shut off the soundtrack. He immediately does so, which gives the demonstration a grotesque and comic appearance as the camera pans across the crowd, finally arriving at the male instructor leading them in the foreground.

It's a deliberate distancing effect that is used no less effectively for noncomic purposes in the final sequence of *Close-up*, when the main character Hossein Sabzian—who has just emerged from prison for impersonating Makhmalbaf, his idol—meets Makhmalbaf for the first time in an encounter arranged by Kiarostami. Sabzian rides on the back of his idol's motorbike to the home of the wealthy family he previously deceived, purchasing a bouquet of flowers on the way as a peace offering. In the latter scene, we're offered the explanation that Kiarostami's sound equipment failed to pick up all the conversation between the two men en route, reportedly either a half-truth or an outright lie that has the same basic effect as the wry pretext for turning off the sound in *Homework:* it is an invitation for the viewer to step back from a climactic scene and reflect. One might even say that the deception in both cases is motivated less by an exposé of the documentary form than by a creative use of it, with an interest in fostering a sense of detachment about what's being shown.

(More recently, at pivotal moments in *The Wind Will Carry Us* and *A.B.C. Africa*, darkness has a function similar to that of silence here.)

Like *Six Degrees of Separation*, with which it has a few striking similarities, *Close-up* is based on the true story. In 1989 an impoverished bookbinder and film freak in his thirties named Sabzian, sitting next to a middle-class housewife named Mrs. Ahankhanh on a bus in Tehran, claimed to be Makhmalbaf. Makhmalbaf was then and is now one of the most famous artists in Iran, a former fundamentalist and guerilla against the shah in his teens who first became a playwright, then an increasingly skeptical and adventurous filmmaker whose best known films by the late 1980s included *The Cyclist* (1987) and *Marriage of the Blessed* (1989). Continuing his impersonation, Sabzian was invited to the woman's home and befriended her husband and two grown sons, offering to cast them all in his next film and proposing to use their house as a location. After borrowing money from the Ahankhanhs that he failed to return, he was eventually exposed as a fraud and arrested.

Ready with a film crew to shoot another feature, Kiarostami read a story about the Sabzian incident in a weekly magazine and immediately decided to shift his plans and make a film about this subject instead, with all the real people playing their own parts in a restaging of some of the events—not only the meeting between Sabzian and Mrs. Ahankhanh on the bus and his subsequent arrest but also Kiarostami's visit to Sabzian in jail, when he asked the bookbinder to play himself in a picture. At the trial, the judge allowed Kiarostami to spend ten hours filming, which undoubtedly expanded and complicated the proceedings. Two cameras were used, one of them reserved for close-ups of Sabzian, the other employing a zoom lens that roved more freely around the courtroom.

In some cases in *Close-up*, including the film's very first scene, major events are restaged from unexpected vantage points: after a reporter from the weekly magazine is alerted that Sabzian is about to be arrested at the Ahankhanhs' home, we accompany him and the two policeman in a cab to the designated house, but once we get there, we perversely remain outside with the driver, who picks flowers from a pile of leaves nearby, dislodging an aerosol can that he distractedly kicks across the road. Sabzian himself is barely visible when he gets into the cab with the two policemen, and it might be argued that the driver, reporter, and even the spray can—later kicked again by the reporter while he searches for a tape recorder at the houses of the Ahankhanhs' neighbors—are more important at this stage of the plot.

Much later in the film, we finally get to see the same scene from the vantage point of the Ahankhanhs and Sabzian inside the house. And still later we're present at a brand new scene arranged by Kiarostami himself, which I've already described: Sabzian, out of jail, meets the real Makhmalbaf for the first time and climbs on the back of his motorbike so they can jointly pay a visit to the Ahankhanhs. The bouquet of flowers that he buys for them echoes the flowers picked by the driver from the pile of leaves in the opening sequence, outside the same house.

The more we watch these events unfold, the more mysterious as well as unexpected everything becomes. In the first scene, the giddiness of the reporter anticipating a scoop is emphasized. We don't get to the restaged meeting of Sabzian and Mrs. Ahankhanh on the bus until the middle of the trial, when it occurs as a sort of impromptu flashback, and even the matter of whether the participants are always furnishing their own dialogue is less than obvious. (The scene looks rehearsed, and assuming that their memories diverge at all, we can't tell whose version of this scene prevails.) Kiarostami generally remains offscreen or viewed from behind, and the degree to which he functions as ringmaster as opposed to simple witness isn't spelled out.

Everything, in short, gets thrown into question; the veracity of what we see and hear remains uncertain, and that's really the point: the closer up we get, the farther away we feel from grasping this simple story with any confidence. For Sabzian, we quickly learn, movies are a matter of life and death, and the reverence for art and poetry held throughout Iranian society—which is partly what made his impersonation possible in the first place—is an important part of what gives *Close-up* its pungency. Film, as we see it here, enables people to cross class barriers, in their imaginations when they watch films and, in this case, in life when a poor man impersonates a famous film director. It becomes an instrument of empowerment as well as a double-edged sword: Sabzian goes to jail for impersonating someone else, but Kiarostami gets prizes and recognition for persuading Sabzian, the Ahankhanhs, the reporter, the judge, and others to impersonate themselves.

| | |

The implied critiques of parents and teachers in *The Traveler* and *Homework* are much more overt in *Where Is the Friend's House?* and the fact that Kiarostami is faulting them in similar ways in the latter film is underlined by the way he uses the classroom and the courtyard outside Ahmad's house as the sites of parallel abuses. A stern male teacher tears up the work of one of Ahmad's classmates, Mohammed, who did not do his homework in his notebook, reducing the boy to tears. Then Ahmad discovers after school that he has inadvertently picked up Mohammed's notebook along with his own, and for most of the remainder of the film he struggles to find Mohammed's house to return it. After failing to do so, he winds up doing Mohammed's homework for him.

Asking directions from strangers is an almost constant theme in Kiarostami's work, starting with this movie, which is often comic and implicitly philosophical as it relates allegorically to life's journey. "How long is a lifetime?" asks the old doormaker while accompanying Ahmad on part of his quest. The doormaker is the only sympathetic adult in the film, and, for better and for worse, he is also an obvious precursor of the Turkish taxidermist in *Taste of Cherry* and the doctor in *The Wind Will Carry Us* as a somewhat sentimentalized receptacle for wisdom in relation to the concerns of the hero.

In contrast to the marked absence of sentimentality elsewhere in these films, these three characters remain somewhat problematical, and I therefore agree with the film critic David Denby's criticism of Kiarostami's uses of the taxidermist and doctor as purveyors of truth; the latter in particular registers like a lazy recourse to an overworked trope. Yet when the same doormaker (or at least the nonprofessional actor playing him) reappears in *Life and Nothing More . . .* , these strictures no longer apply to the same extent. The same figure is now filmed from a greater distance, and he no longer assumes the same role with the same dramatic or moral function: he's carrying a toilet when the hero gives him a lift, and though he still philosophizes, this is less about life in general and more about his objections to the film he appeared in. In response to a query from the director's son that he doesn't seem as hunchbacked as he did in the film, he complains that he was asked to pretend to be a hunchback in the film. "What kind of art is it to show people older and uglier than they are?" he asks rhetorically. "To make an old man a little younger—that's art." We're left with the impression that we don't really know this character very well. We only thought we did—and this is the kind of false knowledge, encouraged by cinema in general, that *Life and Nothing More . . .* obliquely but consistently criticizes.

The difficulty of finding one's way to a given location, which in *Where Is the Friend's House?* is equated with the difficulty of being and remaining ethical, assumes many of the qualities of an epic theme here and throughout much of *Life and Nothing More . . .* and *The Wind Will Carry Us,* though it also significantly becomes the basis for an extended gag at the start of the latter film. The difficult journey is a good example of the way everyday life in Iran can immediately take on poetic or philosophical nuances. During my only visit to the country to date, when I spent eight days in Tehran as a juror at the Fajr Film Festival in 2001, there were few excursions I took with Iranians either by foot or car, apart from the most routine, in which stopping to ask for instructions from strangers didn't become necessary at some point. And because of the way Kiarostami's heroes repeatedly ask themselves, "Where am I?" or "Where am I going?" the more existential questions of "Who am I?" and "What am I doing?" are never far away.

| | |

Perhaps the second most dramatic quantum leap to date in Kiarostami's career, after the one between *First Graders* and *Homework,* is the one between *Where Is the Friend's House?* and *Life and Nothing More. . . .* The latter qualifies as neither a remake nor a sequel in any ordinary sense (and it's important to recall that Kiarostami made two essential works, *Homework* and *Close-up,* during the five-year interval in between), yet it's still a logical and meaningful outgrowth of its predecessor. To a certain extent it could be called a critique, not of *Where Is the Friend's House?* itself but of its use as a habitual reference point, for the viewer and Kiarostami alike. The nameless hero (Farhad Kheradmand) is the director character, a transparent stand-in for Kiarostami, who drives to Koker with a son to find the two boys who played Ahmad and Mohammed, brothers in real life, five days after a devastating, real-life earthquake hit this region of northern Iran. By the end of this film, the director's mission is made to seem virtually irrelevant—

a small, personal window on a disaster that reportedly killed over fifty thousand people.

Kiarostami did spend a morning and afternoon with his son the day after the earthquake in 1990, driving to villages hit by it; five months later he returned with actors playing himself and his son, using his own car, by his own account, to save money. Asked in an interview why he failed to reveal whether the child actors were found (a question he winds up resolving only in *Through the Olive Trees*) he replied that his desire to find the boys was purely personal and to resolve that issue in this film would be sentimental. This probably would have made his film a hit in Iran but would have betrayed his intentions: "You can't forget that over 20,000 children were killed in that earthquake. My two heroes could have been among them."[10]

The closest Kiarostami comes to resolving this issue is toward the end of the film when he shows the hero give a lift to two other boys, one of them a bit player in *Where Is the Friend's House?* whom he barely remembers. The effect of this substitution is subtle yet profound, giving the viewer's imagination more access to the enormity of the event by keeping the resolution of the quest offscreen while showing us two other boys in which we have much less emotional investment. By caring less, we're ultimately enabled to perceive and contemplate a good deal more, including the comic importance of a football game on TV to the hero's son and many survivors.

The discrepancy between the very small and the very large is in fact basic to the film's vision, to the point of becoming translated into the film's mise en scène and découpage (that is, its mise en scène combined with its editing), which constantly moves back and forth between close shots of people and extreme long shots of mountains. (The director Ernst Lubitsch once said that if you start out by filming mountains, you can learn to film people; Kiarostami at times seems to proceed in the reverse manner.) The frequent shifts in scale can even be felt in the metaphorical equation periodically made in the film between car and camera: both are perceived as middle-class instruments of entitlement and access, perception and circumscription. It might even be said that the hero is associated so closely with his Land Rover precisely because he's never shown with a camera; the numerous point-of-view shots from the front of the car in motion effectively make camera and car seem interchangeable. The car, like the (unseen) camera, is the only element in this devastated world that smacks of interiority; this is the first of Kiarostami's features set exclusively in exteriors, but it would not be the last.

The quixotic theme of the hero with an obsessive quest who fails—common to both *Where Is the Friend's House?* and *Life and Nothing More . . .* (as well as all other Kiarostami narrative features with the exception of *Report* and *10* [2002])—is complemented in each case by a displacement of the viewer's narrative expectations. The frustration that this entails is precisely what makes Kiarostami an infuriating filmmaker for some spectators—and an inspiring one for others who accept the displacement as part of a larger education, a route into those many "smaller" and less obvious stories (as well as those "larger" nonnarrative perceptions) that generally exist outside the compulsive continuities of conventional narrative. From a literary standpoint, the digressions are moments drenched in personality, humor, and atmosphere, not unlike some of those found in works by Laurence Sterne and Nikolay Gogol: like the father and son, we set out looking for only two characters and wind up finding a good many others.

Partly for this reason, it might be said that some of Kiarostami's most creative and unorthodox redefinitions of narrative space—which reach an apotheosis in *The Wind Will Carry Us* but are also present in certain scenes of *A.B.C. Africa*—are effectively launched in *Life and Nothing More. . . .* This redefinition entails not only a complex articulation and development of offscreen space but also a certain independence assigned to the sound track so that it's no longer simply an illustrative accompaniment to the image but also on occasion provides a contrapuntal alternative. For instance, a conversation inside the car, beginning with a shot of the characters inside, continues in the "foreground" of the soundtrack while the camera pans away from the car as it nears a curve in the road, moves past a pedestrian near the side of the road, and then rejoins the car as it reenters the shot from the left after rounding the curve. (The juxtaposition of "foregrounded" dialogue with cars moving in long shot is what prompted me to ask Kiarostami in an interview in this volume if he was ever interested in comic strips.) The consequence, which bears more and more fruit in Kiarostami's subsequent work, is to make the world seem like a richer and more complex terrain than any narrative could possibly contain, with Bruegelesque details playing an increasingly important role—not only on the periphery of certain shots but also at the beginning or end of certain lengthy takes, before or after the central narrative thread is continued.

It seems appropriate to call this enrichment and decentering of narrative space Tatiesque, given Tati's approach in *Playtime* (1967); the technique becomes especially apparent in the cosmic (and comic) long shots that occur toward the end of the picture, culminating in the puzzle-like vista of various interactions between the hero's car and a pedestrian moving up a hill and then across the side of it in the film's concluding long take. For this reason, the first question I can recall asking Kiarostami the first time I met him, specifically in relation to *Life and Nothing More . . .*, was what sort of significance Tati's work had for him. He replied that the name wasn't familiar to him, and in fact he hasn't shown any awareness of Tati in any further statements of his that I've encountered.

Some critics have suggested that Kiarostami might be coy about such matters, but I'm more inclined to take him at his word, for several reasons. For one thing, it's obvious that he's anything but a cinephile. Despite an increasing awareness of world cinema that has come from attending many film festivals and sitting on a lot of festival juries, he rarely thinks in terms of film references. Second, he hasn't been reluctant in interviews to describe other filmmakers who have influenced him: he has stressed that Saless, Kimiavi, and Dariush Mehrjui had a much greater impact than Dreyer or Robert Bresson, and in an interview in this volume he volunteers the information that he has more recently studied films by Bresson for their handling of sound. Third, what I'm describing as his Tatiesque compositions start at least as far back as *Orderly or Disorderly*. And ironically yet significantly, I can testify from my own acquaintance with Tati—having worked for him briefly as a script consultant in 1973[11]—that he was far from being a cinephile himself. With both filmmakers, I'd conclude that their partially shared philosophies of sound and image derive more from the similar ways they regard the world, ethically as well as aesthetically, than from their experiences as moviegoers.

Yet with or without Tati's specific influence, the parallels in method and vision between his work and Kiarostami's are too striking to ignore. I've already noted the parallelism that characterizes the filming of various drivers from the same angle with a telephoto lens in both *Fellow Citizen* and documentary segments of Tati's *Trafic*. I might have added

A Tatiesque composition in *Orderly or Disorderly*

that the same technique is used memorably in the opening sequence of *Life and Nothing More . . .*, filmed from a tollbooth (with only the forearms of the attendant visible) and edited so that we have the impression of watching a single continuous take, though in fact eight separate cars and drivers are recorded. (What we hear over this sequence already announces the relative independence of sound from image: radio reports about the earthquake and additional information from the drivers and attendant.)

More generally, there's a decentering of the narrative away from the (putatively) central characters of both *Playtime* and *Life and Nothing More. . . .* Just as Tati takes pains to subvert audience expectations about Hulot as the central focus of *Playtime* via a series of lookalikes (generally known as "false Hulots"), the two boys given lifts near the end of *Life and Nothing More . . .* are false versions of the boys that the hero and, by implication, the audience, is hunting for. Similarly, the director's losing track of his son's whereabouts while each of them is wandering around ruins or chatting with survivors recalls the characters of Hulot and Giffard losing track of one another in office buildings throughout much of *Playtime.*

| | |

Through the Olive Trees is the third film in Kiarostami's so-called Koker Trilogy (a grouping of titles he himself resists), an offshoot of one scene in *Life and Nothing More . . .* between the director and a quarrelsome newlywed couple who got married the day after the earthquake. I must confess that it is the only one of Kiarostami's mature features that I have serious problems with. The first of his European coproductions, reportedly marking his first (and so far only) employment of a professional actor (Mohammad-Ali Keshavarz), it feels more calculated to me than anything else in his oeuvre, with heavy doses of manufactured charisma and folkloric goodwill that remind me of the worst aspects of Makhmalbaf's *Gabbeh* (1996)—that is, the most touristic aspects, which unfortunately also mean the most commercial. It's not so much that I dislike these elements in themselves as I resent their presence in a Kiarostami feature, particularly when they border on class condescension. The quixotic quest of Hossein—the illiterate gofer on the crew of *Life and Nothing More . . .* who gets hired to play the young groom and is determined to marry Tahereh, the high school girl playing his young wife, who won't even acknowledge his existence when they aren't on camera—is too poignant for words. One can certainly see his resemblance to the fourteen-year-old hero of *The Experience* and his broader relation to someone like Sabzian in *Close-up*, yet Kiarostami does not bring much insight to the character. And though the story as a whole has more to do with filmmaking, at least as a process rather than as a state of mind, than anything else in Kiarostami's oeuvre, it also registers as less dialectical or critical than his other forays into cinema as a subject. Much as *First Graders* might be regarded as an unsuccessful first draft of *Homework*, *Through the Olive Trees* can profitably be read, at least in part, as an early study for *The Wind Will Carry Us*, as well as a further development of certain formal notions of relating sound to landscape that were first broached in *Life and Nothing More. . . .*

The mix between fiction and actuality in *Through the Olive Trees* certainly has its intriguing aspects, although one has to know the previous films to understand most of them. Keshavarz and Farhad Kheradmand (playing himself playing the director in *Life and Nothing More . . .*) offer two separate versions of Kiarostami in the same film. The former introduces himself to the camera by name in the opening shot as "the actor who plays the part of the director," adding, "The other actors have been recruited locally," and then speaks about the effects of the local earthquake until he gets pulled away by Mrs. Shiva, his production manager, to audition high school girls for the part of the the young bride.

Many of the crew members on *Through the Olive Trees*, including the assistant director (and future director) Jafar Panahi, play themselves; Hossein plays himself playing Hossein in *Life and Nothing More . . .* (though the part of Tahereh in *Life and Nothing More . . .* was played by someone else entirely) while Ahmad Ahmadpour and Babak Ahmadpour—the brothers in *Where Is the Friend's House?* whom the hero is looking for in *Life and Nothing More . . .*—belatedly reveal that they survived the earthquake by serving as gofers who carry flowerpots to the location of the half-ruined building where Kheradmand, Hossein, and Tahereh play their scene.

All this sounds better than it plays, in part because Tahereh is allowed to function only briefly as a character in two short scenes at the beginning, in both cases without Hossein's presence. The rest of the time, having no words of her own to deliver and most often kept in long shot or else out of camera range—both in the scene she's playing and in Kiarostami's depiction of its filming through many blown takes—she has little opportunity to register as anything but a concept. So, it isn't surprising that the story as a whole feels somewhat predigested. Apart from the film's deliberately puzzling final shot—a cosmic long shot of Tahereh crossing a clump of olive trees and Hossein following her, until he catches up with her in the far distance and then starts running back—this is a film that uncharacteristically asks fewer questions than it should.

Through the Olive Trees is the second Kiarostami feature in a row filmed exclusively in exteriors, yet the sense of a public, social space transacted between poor and middle-class characters in *Life and Nothing More . . .*—with the car serving most often as mediator between the two—is less clearly defined here. In the opening sequence, Keshavarz describes the location as a rebuilt school, but we only faintly discern the facade of a building in the background of one shot; the casting call takes place exclusively outdoors, and the avoidance of interiors seems contrived, perhaps to avoid confronting certain social issues. The half-ruined building where the scene with Kheradmand, Hossein, and Tahereh is shot was already vaguely defined as a dwelling unit for the couple in *Life and Nothing More . . . :* flowerpots on the upper balcony to be watered, shoes hidden behind the lower steps, but no clear space to sleep or eat. Now that it's strictly a film set, Kiarostami underlines the artificiality—having Keshavarz insist on Hossein citing more family losses in the earthquake in his dialogue than he actually suffered—yet this sort of imposture doesn't seem intended to throw any doubts on our viewing the director as a benign Mr. Chips.

Mrs. Shiva, like Behzad in *The Wind Will Carry Us,* often shows an ill-disguised contempt for the local yokels (including Tahereh when she turns up for shooting in an inappropriate nonpeasant dress). Yet Keshavarz basically comes across as a patriarchal sweetiepie in a white beard who disconcertingly evokes Santa Claus, especially around schoolchildren. He dispenses wisdom and advice to Hossein without a trace of irony, even prompting the actor to follow Tahereh on foot in the final sequence. It's true that Hossein teaches him a thing or two about local customs, but Keshavarz never shows any sign of acknowledging this fact. Perhaps the problem also resides in his skills as a professional actor overpowering Hossein Rezai as a nonprofessional—and Kiarostami going along with this imbalance rather than contesting it.

| | |

Taste of Cherry, one of Kiarostami's greatest as well as most controversial films, brought to a head various debates about the meaning and function of the missing pieces in his narratives, especially after it won the Palme d'Or at the Cannes Film Festival in 1997 (which it shared with Shohei Imamura's *The Eel*). Mr. Badii, the fiftyish central character, contemplates suicide and we never learn why; after a day's deliberation and preparation, we don't even know whether he succeeds. It has been widely argued that Kiarostami omits this information because he has, as the cliché goes, nothing to say. I would counter that because he's speaking with and through us—inviting us to share in a collective voice and common narrative—we have to share part of the burden of determining whether in fact the film is saying anything. If we don't want to think about our own deaths and what this reluctance might say about our lives—or about the possible suicides of strangers and how we might respond to their appeals—*Taste of Cherry* can't have much to say to us.

Badii drives around the hilly outskirts of Tehran in search of someone who will bury him if he succeeds in swallowing sleeping pills and who will retrieve him from the hole in the ground he has selected if he fails. Over the course of an afternoon, he picks up three passengers and asks each one to perform this task in exchange for money: a young Kurdish

Mr. Badii in *Taste of Cherry* (courtesy of Mongrel Media)

The Afghan seminari-an in *Taste of Cherry* (courtesy of Mongrel Media)

soldier stationed nearby, an Afghan seminarian who's somewhat older than the soldier, and a Turkish taxidermist who's older than the seminarian. The soldier runs away in fright; the seminarian tries to persuade Badii not to kill himself; and the taxidermist, who also tries to change Badii's mind, reluctantly agrees because he needs the money for medical care of his sick child. The terrain that Badii's Range Rover repeatedly traverses is mainly parched, dusty, and spotted with ugly construction sites and noisy bulldozers, though the site he's selected for his burial is relatively quiet, pristine, and uninhabited. Badii and the taxidermist decide that the taxidermist will come to the designated hillside at dawn, call Badii's name twice, toss a few stones into the hole to make sure Badii isn't sleeping, and then, if there's no response, shovel dirt over his body and collect the money left for him in Badii's parked car.

Later that night, Badii emerges from his apartment, takes a cab to the appointed spot, and lies down in the hole. We hear the sounds of thunder, rain, and the cries of stray dogs. The screen goes completely black. Then, in an epilogue, we see Kiarostami at the same location, in full daylight, with his camera and sound crew filming soldiers jogging in maneuvers in the valley below. Homayoun Ershadi, the actor playing Badii, lights a cigarette and hands it to Kiarostami; Kiarostami announces that the take is over and they're ready for a sound take. The shot lingers over wind in the trees, now in full bloom, and over the soldiers and filmmakers lounging on the hillside between takes, before the camera pans away to a car driving off into the distance. To the strains of Louis Armstrong playing an instrumental version of "St. James Infirmary," the final credits appear.

The epilogue is shot on video—which is part of what makes it startling—and when Kiarostami attended a preview screening at the Art Institute of Chicago's Film Center, one of the first questions he was asked was why he shot the ending on a different kind of film stock. I expected him to respond by correcting the questioner and explaining that the film stock was the same, that it was only the raw texture of the video image that made the image look different. But Kiarostami chose instead to answer the question as if its assumption about the film stock was correct. Why?

At a conference in Paris in 1995, he said, "I believe in a cinema which gives more possibilities and more time to its viewer . . . a half-fabricated cinema, an unfinished cinema that is completed by the creative spirit of the viewer, [so that] all of a sudden, we have a hundred films."[12] Speaking to Kiarostami in an interview included in this volume, the morning after he appeared at the Film Center, I discovered that he meant this literally, not metaphorically, so that seeing the ending of *Taste of Cherry* as something shot on a different stock was perfectly legitimate as far as he was concerned.

When *Taste of Cherry* opened in Italy in a dubbed version, Kiarostami responded to the pleas of many critics and friends to eliminate the film's epilogue by doing precisely that at several cinemas where the film was showing, chiefly, he wrote me later, as a kind of game to see which version audiences preferred. I suspect this must be the closest he's ever come to test marketing, and I was saddened, though not very surprised, to hear that the version without the epilogue was more popular. When he left Italy, his hope and expectation was that both versions would continue to play, but the distributor followed the logic of the test marketing by retaining only the cut version in theaters. I suspect that if most film critics across the world, including ones in the United States and Iran, had their way, the same sentence might be carried out.

For me, though, the epilogue is crucial, and not because it's telling us, "It's only a movie," as many skeptical critics have maintained. At most it's saying, "It's also a movie," which seems more congruent with the less alienated view of cinema found in Iran. But what it's actually *doing* is far more important than what it's *saying*. If Kiarostami had wanted us to empathize only with Badii's suicidal impulses, he might have told us more about the man, but this would have interfered with his desire for us to empathize as well with Badii's three passengers, who know as little about this stranger as we do; it is their dilemma as well as his that the film is concerned with.

Kiarostami's lack of cinephilia, which I've already made much of, becomes an important aspect of his references to cinema. I believe he makes these references not out of any love for the medium but because of his own experience, which is that of a filmmaker. This is why it was important for him to leave out the hoped-for discovery of the boy stars at the end of *Life and Nothing More . . .* and the hoped-for romantic clinch at the end of *Through the Olive Trees*—both traditional movie standbys.

And the most important thing about the joyful finale of *Taste of*

Cherry is that it's the precise opposite of a distancing effect. Though it invites us into the laboratory from which the film sprang and places us on an equal footing with the filmmaker, it does this in a spirit of collective euphoria, suddenly liberating us from the oppressive solitude and darkness of Badii alone in his grave. By harking back to the soldiers who remind us of the happiest part of Badii's life and a tree in full bloom that reminds us of the Turkish taxidermist's own epiphany—though soldiers also signify the wars that made refugees of both the Kurdish soldier and the Afghan seminarian and a tree is where the Turk almost hanged himself—Kiarostami is representing life in all its complexity. He reconfigures elements from the preceding eighty-odd minutes in video to clarify what in their ingredients is real and what's concocted.

Because Kiarostami's recent cinema continues to be essentially a handcrafted one, some sense of how it's generated is important: without a script and with the dialogue usually generated by him working alone with his nonprofessional actors. This methodology only started becoming clear to Saeed-Vafa and me around the time of *Taste of Cherry,* which is partially why I'm explaining it now, However, one can certainly extrapolate its roots in some of his previous films, for instance, when conversations between two characters are filmed and edited in an angle/reverse-angle pattern rather than with both characters appearing in the same frame, which happens fairly often in *Life and Nothing More . . .* and *Through the Olive Trees,* especially in moving vehicles. This technique likely means that Kiarostami himself is filming each of the actors in separate shooting sessions and then editing the results together by eliminating his own lines. (A somewhat comparable technique was used by Godard in the 1960s when he conveyed lines to actors or fired questions at them over small, invisible earphones.)

| | |

During his conversation with the soldier, Badii says, "I had fun when I did my military service. It was the best time of my life. I met my closest friends there, especially during the first six months." He recalls getting up at four in the morning, polishing his boots, and going out on maneuvers with the major, who got him and the others to count aloud; Badii begins to count himself, in a tight whisper. It's the closest he ever comes in the film to a personal confession.

During his conversation with the seminarian, who disapproves of his plans for religious reasons, Badii replies that when you're unhappy, you hurt other people, and hurting other people is a sin. It's the closest he ever comes in the film to justifying his decision to end his life.

During Badii's conversation with the taxidermist—which Kiarostami cuts to in medias res, eliding how they met and how their conversation began—it's the Turk who does most of the talking, explaining how close he came to suicide himself back in 1960, after a fight with his wife. Deciding to hang himself, he carried a rope to a mulberry tree, but before he could complete the deed, he decided to taste a mulberry, then a second, and a third. He looked at the scenery, heard the voices of children, and decided to live. A little later he asks Badii, "Do you want to give up the taste of cherries?"

| | |

Most of the dialogue occurs between Badii and his three passengers, but apart from Ershadi and the actor playing the Turk—who have a brief second meeting outside the museum where the taxidermist works—none of these four actors ever met while the film was being shot. Kiarostami filmed each of them alone, occupying the passenger seat while Ershadi drove and the driver's seat while each of the other actors was a passenger. Like a novelist inhabiting each of his characters, he thus performed, or played, all these people offscreen, soliciting on-screen dialogue and reactions from each actor through various kinds of manipulation.

Though a feature-length French documentary[13] shows Kiarostami's former actors greeting him with obvious respect and affection, there's a troubling ambiguity about such methods that interferes with the image of him as a "simple" humanist. In the case of *Taste of Cherry,* one clear if subliminal effect of working with each actor in isolation is to create a powerful sense of solitude that is felt throughout the film prior to the exhilarating camaraderie of the epilogue, regardless of whether Badii is alone or with someone else. Yet the fact that the film is set exclusively in exteriors, like the two features before it, inflects our sense of solitude with an equally strong and unbroken sense of being in the world. Consequently, though this film unfolds inside the most private space imaginable—the dark recesses of an individual consciousness bidding farewell to life—it perceives life itself almost exclusively in terms of public and social space, which is the space not only of a car on the road but of an audience in the cinema. This places each creative viewer on the same existential plane as the hero, contemplating the prospect of his or her own solitary death in the public space of a theater. And within the same public space, it also places each creative viewer on the same plane as each of the passengers, contemplating the question of how he or she might respond to such an entreaty from a stranger.

Prior to the epilogue, the action is limited to a single day and evening, but gradually this brief span of time comes to represent the expanse of an entire life, with Badii's passengers representing three successive stages in that life. (Their professions are equally evocative, and their nationalities, like the Armstrong song at the end, help spell out how multicultural and international Kiarostami's cinema had become by this time.) Few films are more attentive to the poignancy of time passing and the slow fading of daylight, so that mundane details throughout the day's progress—from the cheerful lifting of Badii's car out of a rut by field workers to a bulldozer emptying dirt and rocks, from a plane's wispy exhaust trail in the sky to a glimpse of schoolchildren running around a track—register increasingly like signs and epiphanies, supercharged morsels of an existence about to be extinguished. And for all the uplift of the epilogue, we don't have to remember all the lyrics of "St. James Infirmary" (which accompanies and concludes it) to know that death is still waiting around the corner.

| | |

Behzad, the hero of *The Wind Will Carry Us*, is an unspecified media person from Tehran who drives with a camera crew of three to a remote Kurdish village, where they secretly wait for an ailing one hundred-year-old woman named Mrs. Malek to die, apparently in order to film or tape an exotic funeral ceremony afterward for which some women mourners scratch and scar their faces. Behzad spends most of the movie biding his time in the village, circulating a false story about the reason for his presence (buried treasure), and chatting with a few locals—mainly a little boy named Farzad who's the old woman's grandson and who serves as his (and our) main source of information about the village.

Whenever Behzad's cellular phone rings, he drives to the cemetery on top of a hill overlooking the village for better reception. (The first call he receives is from his family in Tehran, and we quickly discover that because he is waiting for the old woman's funeral, he has to miss a family funeral; all the subsequent calls are from his woman producer in Tehran.) At the same location he periodically chats with Youssef, a young man digging a deep hole there for unstated "telecommunications" purposes (most likely, an antenna or tower). Behzad tells Youssef more than once how lucky he is not to be working under any boss, and, after glimpsing the retreating figure of the digger's sixteen-year-old fiancée Zeynab, who brings him tea from time to time, Behzad endeavors to meet her in the village by asking to buy some fresh milk from her family.

In the seven-minute sequence occurring roughly halfway through the film that prompts the film's title, Behzad gets directed to a cellar in the village lit only by a hurricane lamp, where Zeynab obligingly milks a cow for him. Over the course of a lengthy take from a stationary camera, Behzad remains offscreen while Zeynab is mainly seen from behind, though we can see her hands milking the cow. During his ensuing small talk, as he idly flirts with her and casually remarks, "I'm one of Youssef's friends. In fact, I'm his boss," he also speaks to her somewhat condescendingly about Forugh. Interspersed with his various comments and questions to her, which she responds to minimally, he also recites one of Farrokhzad's poems, "The Wind Will Take Us Away":

> In my little night, ah
> the wind has a date with the leaves
> in my little night lurks the agony of destruction.
>
> Listen!
> Do you hear darkness blowing?
> I look upon the bliss like a stranger
> I am addicted to my despair.
> Listen!
> Do you hear darkness blowing?
>
> Now something is passing in the night
> the moon is red, and restless
> and over this rooftop
> laden with the fear of crumbling
> clouds resemble a procession of mourners
> waiting for the moment of rain.

A moment
and then nothing,
night shuddering beyond this window
the earth
screeching to a halt,
something unknown watching you and me
beyond this window.

O green from head to foot
place your hands in my loving hands
like a burning memory,
and yield your lips up
to the caresses of my loving lips
like a warming sense of being.
The wind will take us away
The wind will take us away.
(translated by Ahmad Karimi-Hakkak)[14]

It's a scene that echoes Behzad's encounters with an older woman who runs a local cafe and his intrusive photographing of some local women much later; in both cases, his equipment—car or camera—is experienced as a form of invading weaponry. And it's important to note that most of the sequence unfolds in semidarkness. In fact, many major characters in the film—including Mrs. Malek, Youssef, and all three members of Behzad's crew—are never seen at all, and it isn't until the very end of this sequence that we get to see Zeynab's face, in broad daylight, and then only from a distance, after Behzad leaves. (Her refusal to show her face to him, even when he asks her to, is clearly a form of resistance to his aggressive behavior.) Kiarostami's insistence on throwing us back on our own resources—refusing to take us into the village houses, for instance, except for this one scene in the cellar in which we can barely see anything—means that we, along with Behzad, have to become navigators of his elliptical spaces. (In one exterior scene, viewed from a balcony, Behzad's green apple accidentally drops to Farzad on a lower level, rolling this way and that in a magically unpredictable zigzagging trajectory—a graphic pattern that recurs throughout this film, effectively charting out the opening shot as well as the last. Considering the recurrence of such paths and patterns in Kiarostami's work, from the zigzagging path in *Where Is the Friend's House?* to the kicked spray can in *Close-up,* they virtually amount to a directorial signature.)

Noticing the TV antennas scattered through the village helps us to realize that these people are no more beyond the reach of media than the media people are beyond the reach of the village. The key point is that they speak different body as well as verbal languages, occupy different time frames, and utilize power quite differently. For instance, the villagers often deferentially refer to Behzad as "the engineer," and in some ways Kiarostami seems as amused by their automatic respect for him as he is by Behzad's equally automatic indifference to most of their concerns.

So far I've had little to say about the particular ethics of *The Wind Will Carry Us,* which largely consist of Kiarostami reflecting on his own practice as a "media person" exploiting poor people. To broach this matter, we should consider that Behzad may be the closest thing in Kiarostami's work to a critical self-portrait, which makes up entirely for his relative self-glorification in *Through the Olive Trees.* The most obvious marker of this self-critique is Behzad's cruelty when, at one moment of angry frustration on a hilltop, he kicks a turtle onto its back and leaves it stranded helplessly—at least until the turtle manages to regain its footing as Behzad drives back down the hill. But to my mind a far more telling (if appreciably more subtle) moment occurs just before the title sequence, when Behzad is getting Farzad to fetch him a bowl to carry the fresh milk he's about to get from Zeynab, despite the fact that the boy keeps insisting he's too busy and wants to get to back to his work in the fields. The following exchange takes place as the camera cuts back and forth between the two characters:

BEHZAD: Can you answer me frankly?
FARZAD: Yes.
BEHZAD: Do you think I'm bad?
FARZAD: (*smiling*) No.
BEHZAD: Are you sure?
FARZAD: (*assertively*) Yes.
BEHZAD: How can you be sure?
FARZAD: (*blushing a good deal*) I know . . . you're good.
BEHZAD: (*smiling broadly*) Well, since I'm good, can you get me a bowl to carry the milk?

Kiarostami confirmed that he was the one standing behind the camera and asking Farzad these questions (see the interviews in this volume). And the fact that Zeynab is comparably circumspect and reticent about responding to Behzad's teasing and bullying treatment of her is no less telling. (A more trivial self-reflexive thread in the film is the fact that Behzad often has trouble locating his invisible crew; Kiarostami has complained in many interviews about the late rising and frequent unavailability of his cinematographer, Mahoud Kalari, during shooting.)

The point, in other words, is that Kiarostami is critiquing the whole premise of his own filmmaking and implying that there's no ethical difference between a TV director making a documentary about an old woman's funeral and a celebrated filmmaker-artist like himself entering a village to make a feature. But it's worth adding that all his features since *Homework* deal with interactions between relatively empowered figures such as himself, as filmmaker and potential employer, and relatively disempowered working-class people, as potential employees.

It would be oversimplifying matters, however, to claim that Kiarostami presents Behzad simply as a villain. After a scene in which he berates Farzad in a particularly demeaning way, Behzad goes out of his way to apologize to him; and in contrast to his gratuitous cruelty toward the turtle, he later watches the Herculean efforts of a dung beetle pushing its load on the same hilltop with genuine admiration. Though he refuses to sully himself by attempting to dig Youssef out of his hole when the digger becomes buried and nearly suffocates in an accidental cave-in, he drives around frantically enlisting other villagers to carry out this task, and he obviously cares about the fate of his alleged employee. Perhaps the most important thing about him isn't whether he's simply "good" or "bad"—the language of his ambiguous conversation with Farzad—but the different ways he relates to the world around him in contrast to the locals.

| | |

By concentrating on the death of a century-old woman in the year 1999, Kiarostami appears to be making some sort of millennial statement that has probably meant more outside Iran, in relation to the millennial calendars of the West, than it did inside (especially since, when I visited Tehran in early 2001, the film still had not been shown there commer-

The opening of *The Wind Will Carry Us*

cially). And in comically divvying up his world between media "experts" and peasants—moguls with cellular phones and ordinary working people—he's raising the issue of whom this world actually belongs to, both deservedly and in fact.

Is there any more pressing and relevant global issue at the moment? This is the film's major theme, though it isn't the only one. A major theme of *Taste of Cherry*—mortality in general and the state and process of being buried in particular—returns in *The Wind Will Carry Us* as a secondary theme, along with the equally relevant motif of birth. (A human leg bone, functioning as a highly suggestive prop, is found in Youssef's hole and carried around for a spell by Behzad.) And uniting all these themes is the film's use of poetry, featuring lines from Rumi and *The Rubáiyát of Omar Khayyám* as well as Forugh and sometimes functioning ironically, because of their class differences, as what the characters appear to share the most. Finally, there's also the village itself, with all its intricate interweavings, gravitational ambiguities, and slanting declivities—an architectural marvel both as subject and as backdrop.

| | |

I've had the benefit of viewing Kiarostami's ninety-two-minute rough cut of *A.B.C. Africa*, his first digital video, in Tehran as well as his eighty-four-minute final version transferred to thirty-five millimeter film in the United States. It's obvious that this documentary is a departure for him in many ways, being his first feature made outside Iran and his first work that's primarily in English. It's also possibly his most accessible picture to date, confirming that he has become as multinational or as transnational as he is Iranian, which may help to account for his worldwide reputation. But it's also a film that recapitulates certain aspects of *The Wind Will Carry Us,* confirming in a way Kiarostami's contention that fiction and documentary aren't easy to separate. Both films concern—and interrogate, from an ethical perspective—the position of media people from the city arriving in a remote and impoverished village to wait for villagers to die. And both contain scenes set in the darkness that play crucial roles in focusing the film's interrogation while providing the viewer a certain space and time for reflection. The most obvious difference is that *A.B.C. Africa* is a commissioned film made expressly to draw attention to a social crisis, and critics who have complained that Kiarostami's response to this crisis is superficial and inadequate obviously expected a different kind of film from him.

Shot with two cameras by Kiarostami and his assistant, Seifollah Samadian, who also helped with the editing, *A.B.C. Africa* was made at the request of the Uganda Women's Efforts to Save Orphans program, part of the United Nations' International Fund of Agricultural Development. A letter of thanks from the fund's Takao Shibata, dated March 23, 2000, arrives in Kiarostami's fax machine in the opening shot, explaining how civil unrest and AIDS have left Uganda with about 1.6 million children and teenagers who have lost one or both of their parents—and expressing how a film by him might "sensitize people around the world [to] the devastating dimensions of this tragedy."

As a fulfillment of this assignment, *A.B.C. Africa* initially seems to have scant relation to Kiarostami's earlier films, apart from many shots of landscapes from moving cars and the frequent visibility of Kiarostami. Furthermore, the emphasis on orphans joyously singing and dancing, which was even greater in the rough cut, predictably has raised questions with skeptical viewers. The essential facts, most often conveyed through on-screen or offscreen interviews with women who take care of the children, are never shirked or glossed over, and one unforgettable sequence is set inside a hospital. But this film, with its uncanny kinship at times to Hollywood musicals in terms of bold colors, mobility of camera and actors, and sheer energy, is as much a celebration of the children's inner resources as it is an exposure of their plight. For a filmmaker who for some time has been restricting his use of music to final sequences, this film is a significant departure, and Kiarostami told me he made it in this style because singing and dancing is to a large degree what he encountered among these children.

The impromptu nature of the shoot is made apparent by the fleet movements, hesitations, and shifting paths of the digital video cameras as Kiarostami and Samadian follow, anticipate, or catch up with various children. But the sound mix often emphasizes a contrapuntal rather than an illustrative relation between what we see and what we hear, with the voices of interview subjects frequently becoming disembodied. One of the most unsettling moments in the film occurs in the hospital, when the cries of a boy in pain become detached from the boy himself as we proceed down a hallway, then become overtaken by adult laughter, which in turn becomes disembodied. The discontinuity of emotions in adjacent parts of a hospital is of course unremarkable in itself, but it's hard to think of many filmmakers emphasizing it to the degree that Kiarostami does here. Throughout the film, in fact, one can see him oscillating sharply between inquisitive and emotional responses to his subject. The fact that a celebratory mode emphasizing the children's resilience tends to dominate the emotional responses can be interpreted either as an evasion or as a strategic philosophical position on his part; most likely it's some of both.

Indeed, over the film's second half, the apparent artlessness proves to be deceptive; this is unmistakably a Kiarostami work, albeit one that makes a few bold moves in redefining his art. And the fact that it's a video is part of that redefinition. Kiarostami has made it clear that he wanted to switch to digital video for an ethical reason: the desire to interfere as little as possible with the people he shoots. And though he's still getting used to video technology, which caused delays in the editing, Kiarostami has shown no signs thus far of ever wanting to switch back to film. I expected this new position to entail a fresh aesthetic, yet he seems to have proceeded on the premise that *A.B.C. Africa* is simply a "film" made with more portable equipment, and thus he is in a more equitable relationship with the people he shoots. The only video technique I noticed was the presence of quick, almost subliminal lap dissolves in the final sequence, between clouds seen from a plane and briefly glimpsed black-and-white photos of orphans. (Originally, this sequence was accompanied by a Haydn piece; then the sounds of the plane could be heard over faint traces of the "Blue Danube" waltz; Kiarostami finally wound up overtly opting for the inquisitive over the celebratory mode by removing the latter in the final transfer.)

Insofar as both *Taste of Cherry* and *The Wind Will Carry Us* are about the isolation of the hero from his surroundings, both films, bearing Kiarostami's editing tricks in mind, can also be regarded as complex self-critiques exploring the issue of privileged filmmakers shooting poor people. When I suggested this notion to him during a conversation about *A.B.C. Africa,* he was quick to correct me regarding Ugandans: "Not poor inside." Yet the documentary again makes this critique explicit by emphasizing the presence of not only Kiarostami and Samadian but also the ritzy hotel where they're staying. Furthermore, the periodic freeze-frames of Ugandans, accompanied by the sounds of snapshots being taken, emphasizes the degree to which the film takes an avowedly touristic stance toward its subject. A dialogue between the filmmakers that begins in the darkness outside this hotel, by virtue of being in Farsi, belatedly reminds us that this is, after all, an Iranian video in some respects, such as its philosophically and spiritually inflected humanism.

After more darkness, along with lightning, thunder, and rain, the dialogue resumes the next morning in a half-ruined house occupied by a large family. Though I miss the lovely version of "Autumn Leaves" by a male singer and guitar used during this scene in the rough cut—eventually omitted by Kiarostami because the tune was too familiar—the faintly heard stringed instrument replacing it is certainly more subtle, and this segment remains the work's lyrical climax, with a mood of melancholy hope recalling *Life and Nothing More. . . .*

Our introduction in English to a white Austrian couple adopting an orphaned baby girl broaches the question of what this video might mean to the West—a question brought to the forefront in the closing sequence, when the couple and child board a plane for Austria and we're encouraged to wonder what will happen to all three once they step off the plane at the other end. The fact that we don't see Kiarostami and Samadian as fellow passengers means that *A.B.C. Africa* has by this time effected a quiet and permanent gear change from nonfiction to fiction, with the role of moral witness passing subtly from filmmakers to us. This modulation tactfully brings up the question of our ultimate role in these proceedings, which is a fairly unobtrusive way of achieving the goal assigned to Kiarostami in the opening fax.

| | |

After beginning this study with an evocation of the only Iranian filmmaker I find more poetically powerful than Kiarostami, I'd like to end it with a brief discussion of the most powerful political Iranian film I've seen, *The Circle* (2000). This is the third feature made by possibly the most gifted of Kiarostami's disciples, Panahi, who worked as an assistant director on *Through the Olive Trees* and got Kiarostami to write the screenplay for his first feature, *The White Balloon* (1995). Panahi can be credited with going beyond his mentor in at least one major respect: by giving a particular political thrust to the same kind of narrative ellipsis and deliberate formal construction that Kiarostami is famous for.

As one example, some of the central women characters in the film are fresh out of prison, but we never find out why any of them went to jail in the first place; our understanding in some cases of whether they escaped, were paroled, or simply reached the end of their sentences is either delayed or remains incomplete. We gradually come to realize that none of this information matters, given the story Panahi has to tell, and that our lack of certainty about these details even adds a particular edge to our engagement with the storytelling.

It's an edge that qualifies as an ideological inflection once we realize that this movie refuses to let us rationalize with any excuses or alibis the way these women are treated by their society. The film lacks villains or heroes, because the protagonists all have their lifelike mixtures of strength and weakness. But it's obvious from the outset that what these women have to put up with is intolerable, and Panahi refuses to allow us to say at any point, for any reason, that any of them is "getting what she deserves." As in Kiarostami's films, the narrative gaps here constitute a form of respect for us, but in this case the respect is not merely for our imagination but also for our ethics, our innate sense of decency.

Can Kiarostami be faulted for not making a film as political and as radical as *The Circle*? I think it would be overly critical to do so, considering how comprehensively he has shown Panahi and others what a cinema of this kind might consist of. Even if he has led the way toward a promised land without entering it himself, he has empowered us by providing us with a road that all of us might travel down—a road, snaking off into the distance, that has already circled the globe.

Notes

1. Mehrnaz Saeed-Vafa, "Sohrab Shahid Saless: A Cinema of Exile," in *Life and Art: The New Iranian Cinema,* ed. Rose Issa and Sheila Whitaker (London: National Film Theatre, 1999), 135–44.

2. Godfrey Cheshire, "Confessions of a Sin-ephile: *Close-up," Cinema Scope,* no. 2 (Winter 2000): 3–8.

3. Mohsen Makhmalbaf, "Makhmalbaf Film House," *The Day I Became a Woman* (bilingual ed. of screenplay), trans. Babak Mozaffari (Tehran: Rowzaneh Kar, 2000), 5.

4. Michael C. Hillmann, *A Lonely Woman: Forugh Farrokhzad and Her Poetry* (Washington, D.C.: Three Continents Press/Mage Publishers, 1987), 43 (quote), see also 42–44.

5. The film's producer, Ebrahim Golestan (born 1922)—also a major and pioneering filmmaker in his own right, as well as a novelist and translator—was Farrokhzad's friend and lover for the last eight years of her life, and before making her own films she worked with him as a film editor, most notably on *A Fire,* an account of a 1958 oil well fire near Ahvaz. She studied film production as well as English during a brief visit to England in 1959 and later traveled to Khuzestan and worked on films there as actress, producer, assistant, and editor. According to Karim Emami, who worked for Golestan during this period, Farrokhzad's first experience in handling a movie camera was shooting streets, oil wells, and petroleum pumps in Agha-Jari, from the interior of a touring car, with a super-8 camera—an image evoking Kiarostami's *Taste of Cherry.* Emami adds that Farrokhzad "assisted Golestan in directing" *The Suitor,* the Iranian episode in a National Film Board of Canada production about the rites of betrothal in four countries. She also acted in the episode, though not as the bride or fiancée. (According to other sources, she also acted in a film called *The Sea* and codirected *The View of Water and Fire* in 1961.) After *The House Is Black,* she made "a short commercial for the classified ads page of Kayhan newspaper," which Emami regards as relatively inconsequential. (See Emami, "Recollections and Afterthoughts," an undated lecture delivered in Austin, Texas, <http://www.forughfarrokhzad.org>.) Another detail that seems worthy of mention: the Italian director Bernardo Bertolucci, whom she met in Pesaro, came to Iran in 1966 to make a documentary about her for Italian television.

6. See, for instance, the film's entry in Jamal Omid, *Tarikh-e Cinema-ye Iran* (History of Iranian cinema) (Tehran: Entesharat-e Rozaneh, 1995), 847.

7. Most of this chronology comes from Abbas Kiarostami's "Le monde d'A.K.," *Cahiers du cinéma,* no. 493 (July–Aug. 1995), a French translation of autobiographical statements drawn principally from the monthly Iranian magazine *Mahnameh-ye Film,* currently known as *Film,* founded in 1983. See also Abbas Kiarostami, *Photographies, Photographs, Fotografie . . .* (Paris: Editions Hazan, 1999). This is an excellent collection with an interview and a short biographical sketch.

8. I'm indebted to James Naremore for this insight.

9. Gilberto Perez, "History Lessons," *The Material Ghost: Films and Their Medium* (Baltimore: Johns Hopkins University Press, 1998), 266–70 (quote on 266). The offending article: Jonathan Rosenbaum, "Lessons from a Master," *Chicago Reader,* June 14, 1996, 45–47. This, the third article I devoted to Kiarostami in the *Chicago Reader* after pieces on *Life and Nothing More . . .* ("Iranian Sights," October 23, 1992) and *Homework* and *Through the Olive Trees* ("From Iran with Love," September 29, 1995), was, ironically, written around the same time I was urging Perez, a friend, to see Kiarostami's films.

10. Abbas Kiarostami, *Abbas Kiarostami: Textes, entretiens, filmographie complète,* Petite Bibliothèque des Cahiers du cinéma (Paris: Cahiers du cinéma, 1997), 41–42 (my translation).

11. See my articles "The Death of Hulot," *Placing Movies: The Practice of Film Criticism* (Berkeley: University of California Press, 1995), 163–79, and "Tati's Democracy," *Movies as Politics* (Berkeley: University of California Press, 1997), 37–40.

12. Kiarostami, *Abbas Kiarostami,* 71.

13. Jean-Pierre Limosin, *Abbas Kiarostami: Vérités et mensonges,* in *Cinéma de notre temps* (AMIP, La Sept Arte, INA, 1994, SECAM video).

14. Forugh Farrokhzad, "The Wind Will Take Us Away," *Remembering the Flight: Twenty Poems by Forugh Farrokhzad* (bilingual ed.), trans. Ahmad Karimi-Hakkak (Port Coquitlam, Canada: Nik Publishers, 1997), 25, 27. For alternate translations see "The Wind Will Blow Us Away," *Bride of Acacias: Selected Poems of Forugh Farrokhzad,* trans. Jascha Kessler and Amin Banini (Delmar, N.Y.: Caravan Books, 1982), 23–24, and "The Wind Will Carry Us," trans. David L. Martin, *Film Comment,* July–Aug. 2000, 25.

Abbas Kiarostami

Mehrnaz Saeed-Vafa

I first met Abbas Kiarostami at a screening of *Report* (1977), his first full-length feature, at the Farabi Cinema Club in Tehran in 1977, two years before the Revolution. *Report* is a stark, realistic film that reflects the bleak, mundane life of a government employee alienated from his job, from the social life around him, and from his wife. Mr. Firuzkuhi, the main character of the film, gets fired from his job and, following a few domestic disputes with his wife that culminate in her suicide attempt, leaves her behind in the hospital. Every scene in the film signifies a degree of mental isolation and alienation on the part of Mr. Firuzkuhi. At the time, I liked the film's political tone and the way it showed the cultural alienation during the shah's rule, but I found its treatment of domestic violence, however elliptical, disturbing.

I had just returned from London, eager to make films in Iran. At the suggestion of Bahman Farmanara, director of the award-winning *Prince Ehtejab* (1973) and my former teacher at the School of Television and Cinema, where I had studied for a year and a half in Tehran before leaving for London, I started working on a couple of films, including one of his, *The Tall Shadows of the Wind* (1978). He was the president of a production company that had produced films, including *Report,* by many independent and first-time directors.

In the mid-1970s, my ideal filmmaker was Robert Bresson, whose films I had discovered in London. His sparse and intense yet quiet language and his world of imprisoned characters made a more profound impression on me than that left by any other important director at the time (such as Michelangelo Antonioni, Ingmar Bergman, Federico Fellini, Luis Buñuel, Orson Welles, or Alfred Hitchcock). Bresson became an artistic and poetic reference by which I measured other films. His *Au hasard Balthazar* (1966), *Mouchette* (1967), and *Une femme douce* (1969) showed his profound awareness of and sympathy for women as victims of male possessiveness and violence. This was a highly important topic to me that I had not seen in the works of any other significant filmmaker at the time. When I returned to Iran in 1977, I wrote a long article about his films that was published in a major Iranian film periodical.[1] Bresson ruled my artistic life until I discovered Sergei Paradjanov about a decade later.

At that time the only Iranian films that I admired were Parviz Kimiavi's *P for Pelican* (1970), Sohrab Shahid Saless's *Still Life* (1975), and Forugh Farrokhzad's *The House Is Black* (1962). I had heard a good many admiring comments about Kiarostami and *Report* through my friends who had worked with him, Ahmad Mirshekari (his assistant) and Mahvash Sheikh Ol-Islami (his production manager). They raised my expectations of *Report* so high that I was prepared to be taken by it, but it made a profound negative impression on me: it was too dark for my feminist idealism. The film had a strong, cold, and impersonal tone—a tone similar to that of his remarkable *Taste of Cherry* (1997). Only after getting to know Kiarostami's other work did I start to look at the film differently.

I next saw *The Wedding Suit* (1976), a short feature that is a more literal and matter-of-fact film. The film looked critically at the social conditions of three boys in a working-class business district of Tehran. It is another subtle political attack on the class-conscious culture of the shah's era, including the importance of appearance. The story line is very simple: a suit is made to order for a young middle-class boy to attend a wedding. The suit becomes the object of desire for two poor boys who work in the same building, one of whom borrows it and gets into trouble as a consequence. Although the issues raised in the film (such as class and the exploitation of children) are, like those in *Report,* serious and disturbing, it has a much more conventional plot-oriented structure; the tone is lighter and much more humorous; and it lacks the earlier film's dark, claustrophobic space.

I got a second chance to meet Kiarostami during the early 1980s, at the beginning of the eight-year war between Iran and Iraq. This time we met at Kanun, where I had started making a short film, *The Transfigured Night* (1979). Because of the war, I had to stop shooting, which created a major conflict with my producer. Every week, anxiously, I would go to Kanun to resolve the issue of my unfinished film, and I would see Kiarostami in the hallways, always with a warm, carefree smile and his customary big, dark glasses. It was the image I carried of him for years.

After the Revolution, when cinema was under scrutiny and many major filmmakers had been gone from the country for a decade or more, Kiarostami remained and kept a low profile. I heard that he was doing carpentry and designing and building boxes as well as making a few modest films that later took on more significance. I heard that he also made the controversial *Case No. 1, Case No. 2* (1979)—a film I had to wait twenty years to see because it was banned in Iran.

Meanwhile, after starting out in the United States as a freelance film editor and producer, I began teaching film full-time at Columbia College in Chicago. Shortly afterward, I proposed showing films from Iran at the Art Institute of Chicago's Film Center, at a time when Iranian cinema had not yet made its full international impact, and Barbara Scharres, director of the Film Center, gave me a go-ahead. The next time I met Kiarostami, and my subsequent exposure to his cinema, was in 1992 at the Toronto International Film Festival, eight years after I had left Tehran for Chicago. The festival was showing several Iranian films including three by Kiarostami: *Where Is the Friend's House?* (1986), *Close-up* (1990), and *Life and Nothing More. . .* (1992). (It was only later that I caught up with *Homework* [1988], made between the first two.) Also in Toronto, I asked Jonathan Rosenbaum to see the first of these films, which launched our dialogue about Iranian cinema in general and Kiarostami in particular. And I had my first chance to interview Kiarostami.

| | |

Before the Revolution, political cinema in Iran was targeted against the shah's system of government and Western exploitation and often took the form of attacking Tehran, the capital city, whose dominant culture is often seen to represent the current regime. In Kiarostami's films, Tehran is almost always associated with corruption, as in *Recess* (1972),*The Wedding Suit, Report,* and even *The Traveler* (1974), although the hero's dream in this last film is to go there. In Kiarostami's postrevolutionary films apart from the documentaries, the heroes find refuge from Tehran in rural nature. After the Revolution, the war with Iraq became a focus of political analysis in Iranian cinema. One consequence of this was the emergence of "sacred defense" films that promoted martyrdom and sacrifice to safeguard revolutionary values. But after a few years and a good many casualties a different kind of film appeared, exemplified by Mohsen Makhmalbaf's *The Marriage of the Blessed* (1989) and Ebrahim Hatamikia's *From Kharkheh to Rhine* (1992), that questioned the war and its effects on the populace.

Makhmalbaf's films in this period, including *The Peddler* (1986), were strong critical and despairing statements that protested corruption in postrevolutionary Iran. As their titles suggest, his *Salaam Cinema* (1994) and *Once Upon a Time, Cinema* (1994) both addressed film; the former viewed it as a pretext for authoritarian manipulation and the latter focused on power and state censorship arising from this manipulation. He remains the most controversial filmmaker in Iran because of these films, his private film school (attended mainly by his immediate family), and his fundamentalist past.

Kiarostami's *Close-up* addresses the mythical figure of Makhmalbaf—a former poor man and Islamist rebel imprisoned by the shah—who at the height of his popularity winds up serving as the ideal role model for Sabzian, an unemployed print shop worker who capitalizes on his resemblance to Makhmalbaf by impersonating him to con a wealthy family. *Close-up* shows how cinema, the most popular form of entertainment in Iran, has become perceived as a means to access power overnight (like basketball for American blacks)—a kind of work that requires no education and just a little luck.

Women, both as filmmakers and as subjects, also have been an im-

Hossein Sabzian (*left*) in *Close-up* (courtesy of Mongrel Media)

portant presence in the political context of Iranian cinema over the past decade. Toward the end of the war, two especially significant women filmmakers entered cinema. Rakhshan Bani-Etemad and Tahmineh Milani, with films like *Nargess* (1991) and *Two Women* (1998), brought the plight of women to the screen, replacing the previous preoccupation with young boys. Many male directors have subsequently focused on women as well, culminating in Jafar Panahi's *The Circle* (2000). (More recently, Samira Makhmalbaf and her stepmother, Marzieh Meshkini, have made inroads with *The Apple* (1997) and *The Day I Became a Woman* (2000).In such a climate, one can see why Kiarostami's films have been considered apolitical by some Iranians; I also have reservations about the treatments of the wife in *Report* and the children in *Homework* (1988). I am similarly concerned that Kiarostami got Mohammad-Reza Nematzadeh to cry in *Where Is the Friend's House?* by tearing up a Polaroid picture he liked[2] (I should add that such treatments are far from exclusive to Kiarostami, who is actually less culpable than many others).

In my several trips back to Iran I have interviewed many film critics, friends, and regular viewers about Kiarostami's cinema (I even saw *The Wind Will Carry Us* [1999] a second time in a public theater at the Fajr Film Festival to observe audience reactions, and I found it surprisingly popular, especially with young viewers). As with many other groundbreaking directors, local responses have been divided. Some Iranians call Kiarostami's work uncinematic, journalistic, and unworthy of all the international attention it has received. He himself has been called a favorite of Western festivals who makes films for foreign audiences (which is why they were among the first to discover him), opportunistic, and cowardly (his films have been compared to safety matches). One Iranian told me that Saless, the filmmaker Kiarostami was copying, deserved all the attention; another maintained that Bahram Bayzaie, a scholar of Iranian cinema who was deprived of permission to make films for several years, was entitled to the awards. Others have even suggested that the French and Iranian governments conspired to give Kiarostami so much attention, that his awards were political prizes to buy a good image for Iran, and that Kiarostami had sold himself to the Islamic government to gain fame. They argued that local stupidity had joined the international stupidity that celebrates him and that in Iran he was given carte blanche to do what he wanted, to use any facilities he required, and to employ the resources of Kanun at the cost of depriving others who were more deserving of access to the same resources.

However, no other Iranian filmmaker has influenced as many Iranian features as Kiarostami, thematically and stylistically as well as in terms of their aspirations of international success. There is a school of Kiarostami in Iranian cinema consisting of films by former assistants such as Panahi (*The White Balloon* [1995]), Bahman Ghobadi (*A Time for Drunken Horses* [2000]), and Hassan Yektapanah (*Djomeh* [2000]); by other disciples such as Ali-Reza Raissian (*The Journey* [1995]), Ahmad Talebi (*Willow and Wind* [1999]), and Ibrahim Forouzesh (*The Key* [1986]); and by colleagues such as Farmanara (*The Smell of Camphor, the Fragrance of Jasmine* [2000]), Alireza Davoudnezhad (*Sweet Agony* [1999]), and Mohsen Makhmalbaf (*A Moment of Innocence* [1999]).

I think that Iranian filmmakers should be thankful to Kiarostami for promoting Iranian cinema across the globe and paving the way for others. Other filmmakers before him—directors like Saless, Amir Naderi,

Bayzaie, and Dariush Mehrjui—won awards in festivals, but none has been as consistently successful or famous on the same scale. At a time when Iranians had such a negative image in the West, his cinema introduced a humane and artistic face. I have been enjoying conversations about his cinema with my students and with audiences at Chicago's Film Center for the past decade, and I have been pleased to find them inspired by it. Many second-generation Iranian American students have turned to filmmaking because of him. Also, some of my best and most talented American students have used his films as models for their own work. How can I regard this popularity and success as the result of a conspiracy between governments or the stupidity of the critics? If even the youth of other cultures are inspired by Kiarostami's films, then his cinema has crossed national borders and become universal.

Finally, some of the criticism against his cinema by Iranians inside and outside Iran stems from a general lack of respect for Iranian cinema. While a commercial film enjoys a budget of $20–$200 million, a low-budget Iranian film may look technically threadbare, unglamorous, and far from slick in comparison.

And on a personal note, I would like to express my gratitude toward Kiarostami, who has shown me how to achieve a lot with so few visual means. I respect his cinema immensely. His unique style and humor are simple but radical, poetic, and philosophical. The more I view his films, the more I learn from them.

The Kiarostami films that I saw in Toronto in 1992 were the same three that established his reputation in the West. *Where Is the Friend's House?* which set the themes of his subsequent films much as *A Simple Event* (1973) did for Saless, was inspired in part by "Address," a famous poem by Sohrab Sepehry:

> In the false-dawn twilight
> the rider asked,
> "Where is the House of the Friend?"
> the sky
>   halted
> a passer-by
> had a branch of light
> in his mouth which he gave
> to the darkness of the sand

and pointed with his finger
to an aspen and
said:
"before you get to the tree
there's a garden-lane
more green than God's dream.
and in that garden-lane,
as far as the breadth of the wing-spread
of candor, love is blue.
you go to the end of that lane
which appears behind adolescence
then you turn
towards the flower of solitude
two steps more to the flower . . .
at the foot of the fountain
of eternal earth myths you stop and stay
and a transparent fear envelops you.
in the intimacy of flowing space
you hear a rustling
you see a child
who has climbed up a pine tree
to pick up a chick
from the nest of light.
and from the child you ask:
'where is the House of the Friend?'"[3]

Two scenes in the film impressed me in particular. In the first, when Ahmad, the boy hero, is on his way home from his unsuccessful search for his friend's house, he encounters the hypocrisy and indifference of his elders to his concerns. To assert his authority, his grandfather orders him to get him a pack of cigarettes that he doesn't even need, and a salesman haggling over the price of a door rips out a page of the boy's notebook to do his calculations.

In the second, penultimate scene, Ahmad's long day's failed journey down a zigzagging path to find his friend's home culminates in an image of his mother in the dark. Late at night, Ahmad decides to do his friend's homework for him. A storm blows open the door behind him, revealing his mother handling sheets on the clothesline and thereby connecting her late-night "homework" with his. His anxious response to

The penultimate scene in *Where Is the Friend's House?*

her as she appears and disappears behind the sheets creates a poetic question that the film never answers: Is he afraid of the storm, the darkness outside, or his mother's angry disapproval of him doing another boy's homework? The mysterious eroticism of this scene, recalling some lines in Forugh's "Green Illusion" ("What peak, what summit? / don't these diverse, meandering paths / all end in that cold, all-devouring mouth?"[4]) anticipates the dialogue in the dark cellar in *The Wind Will Carry Us.* (It's interesting to note that while working on this essay, I discovered that an Internet search for the phrase "Where is the friend's house?" in both Persian and English leads to a Web site for Iranian gay men.)

Life and Nothing More . . . is simple but profound. The film begins with an overwhelming sense of tragedy seldom seen in a postrevolutionary Iranian film. The theme is the magnitude of the mass destruction caused by the 1990 earthquake that shook northern Iran. Images of the broken roads, food stores, houses, and cars under the debris and of the people who are digging out the survivors in the noisy atmosphere of helicopters, loudspeakers, and radio news broadcasts add to the post-apocalyptic setting.

Shortly after, these images lead to those of a serene landscape of a remote village in which we hear the sound of mourning villagers in the cemetery, with overlapping baroque music and an attention to the surrounding nature that establishes Kiarostami's point of view. The film evokes images of the Iran-Iraq war, another recent disaster that brought heavy human casualties. A filmmaker with his young son is looking for the two boys who starred in his previous film, asking for their whereabouts and thereby aligning himself with their own search for survivors. But unlike them, he remains an observer who takes us on a tour.

At the time, I thought Kiarostami may have reached his artistic peak. But then I saw *Close-up*.

| | |

> What can I do?
> I talk yet no one hears me
> I see thousands of people who are myself
> Yet they keep thinking they are themselves.
>
> —Rumi[5]

> INTERVIEWER: Is *The Wind Will Carry Us* an image of yourself?
> KIAROSTAMI: Yes, but you have to look for this image in the main character. I also see myself in the little boy. In *Close-up* I find myself in the character of Ali Sabzian and in the Ahankhah family who are deceived. I'm like the character who lies, and at the same time I'm similar to the family who's been lied to. In all films, some characters are like the director, and in *The Wind Will Carry Us,* the woman in the café is like me, although she's a woman.
>
> —*Gozaresh-e Film,* 1999

As *Close-up* begins, we see a frantic reporter picking up two policemen. As they get into the car, the reporter starts talking about arresting a man who has been impersonating Makhmalbaf, the famous Iranian director, to convince a local Turkish family to help him make a film. The reporter's excitement is met with the indifference of the laid-back policemen and the preoccupied driver—an unemployed air force pilot who, by his own account, knows nothing about cinema. They make several stops to ask for directions to the family's house, eventually arriving at an affluent neighborhood in Tehran's north side. (It may puzzle non-Iranian viewers that the reporter and not the police runs the show, but this piece of reality is integral to the film.)

The reporter goes into the house after the policemen ask him to get the impersonator's I.D. and food ration book, leaving us with the others long enough to get some information about who they are and where they come from. A moment later, the reporter comes back to get the policemen and they all go into the house, leaving us behind the closed door with the driver, who has to wait for them.

Like the frustrated Mongols in *The Mongols* (1973)—a feature by Kimiavi, the Iranian New Wave Godard of the 1970s—who are locked behind a door in the middle of a desert, doubtful about the credibility of the director and his cinema, the audience of *Close-up* might experience frustration with Kiarostami. They might want to ask, What is this cinema? Here the audience wants to follow the action—to go into the house with the policemen and reporter—but is kept hostage outside the house to reluctantly watch and share the trivial activities of the driver waiting in this quiet neighborhood. He looks at the sky, picks a couple of roses from a pile of garbage next to his car (a nice motif touching on notions of class and sentimentality), and kicks an empty spray can that we watch roll down the street. What? An empty spray can instead of a dramatic scene?

Here, in the manner of a news report equating a tragic event with an unimportant event, Kiarostami places the dramatic story of the accused man alongside the story of a common man doing nothing of consequence,whose time is, apparently in terms of screen time, more important than the time of the reporter, the main character, or the audience who has paid to watch. Why are we waiting? Isn't our time more valuable than that of the driver doing nothing important?

These are the first ten minutes of *Close-up*, a film that changed the entire course of Iranian cinema. It combines a reenactment with real documentary footage; it is a film based on a real story and acted by the real people involved who play themselves in real locations. It moves and challenges the audience in every direction. This short introductory scene, a microcosm of the Kiarostami universe, contains the very essence of his cinema.

| | |

Kiarostami belongs to the generation of Iranian filmmakers—Forugh, Fereydun Rahnama, Farrokh Ghaffari, Ebrahim Golestan, Kamran Shirdel, Saless, Bayzaie, Kimiavi, Naderi, and Mehrjui—who emerged in the 1960s and flourished in the 1970s. They helped develop an artistic and socially conscious cinema, later known as the Iranian New Wave, that brought new visions and style to cinema and inspired future generations of filmmakers.

Despite political oppression, the 1970s in many respects was a productive artistic period in Iran not only in filmmaking but also in poetry and literature. The Iranian New Poetry blossomed during this period with the emergence of poets like Mehdi Akhavan Saless, Ahmad Shamlou, and Sepehry and with the continuation by Forugh and many others of the movement initiated by Nima Yushij. Several agencies established and invested in film production, which helped the growth of both documentaries and feature films. The most important of these agencies included state-run Iranian National Television, the Ministry of Art and Culture, Kanun, and the Company for the Development of the Iranian Cinema Industry (Sherkat-e Gostaresh-e Sanaye Sinamaye Keshvar); other state agencies including the Oil Company; and many private film companies. Iranian filmmakers and audiences began to see foreign films uncensored and in their original languages—subtitled instead of dubbed into Persian—at the Tehran International Film Festival, which was established in the early 1970s. This exposure helped boost the Iranian public's enthusiasm for film and supported the translation and publication in Iran of several books and periodicals about cinema. At the same time, foreign filmmakers and critics were able to familiarize themselves with Iranian cinema.

For traditional Iran, the surreal, highly modern Shiraz Art Festival—part of the shah's plan to modernize and Westernize Iran and to open the "Gate to Great Civilization" to Iranians—was another important annual event from 1968–1978. Its international program included major works by modern and avant-garde as well as classical performance artists, musicians, filmmakers, and theater directors (Jerzy Grotowsky, Peter Brook, Morris Bejar, Karlheinz Stockhausen, Shuji Terayama), although later it was boycotted by progressive artists to protest the shah's repressive practices. In addition to the Shiraz Art Festival, a costly celebration of 2500 years of monarchy that occurred during the most volatile times of the shah and the Savak (his secret police), accelerated both his downfall and the growth of many movements in Iran that politicized Iranian artists and filmmakers.

For the first time, from the mid-1960s to the mid-1970s, a generation of Iranians who had studied cinema abroad, including Sohrab Shahid Saless, Kimiavi, Farmanara, Hajir Dariush, Ghaffari, and Shirdel, returned home to make films and contribute to a new Iranian cinema. Also, some local filmmakers who had either studied film in Iran or entered cinema from other disciplines were instrumental in the formation and growth of the new cinema. These locals included Kiarostami, Golestan, Mehrjui, Naderi, Naser Taghvaie, Parviz Sayyad, Ali Hatami, Masud Kimiae, and the most significant cultural figure in Iran, the influential writer, cultural scholar, and dramatist Bayzaie, who also is one of the most respected figures of the contemporary Iranian cinema and theater.

The majority of the Iranian films of the 1960s and 1970s were political films that criticized the government and its social system as well as the Western exploitation of Iran. The tone of many of these films was negative, conveying a sense of disappointment and estrangement toward the indifferent and hypocritically imposed modernism of the 1970s. By being cynical and portraying despair, the artists protested the shah's system of positive image propaganda. Good examples of this cinematic cynicism include *The Journey* (1972), *The Cow* (1969), and *Brick and Mirror* (1965). Also notable are the dark portrayal of the life of a government employee in *Report* and the noneventful life of a poor old couple in rural Iran in Saless's *Still Life*.

The cinematic styles of the films varied. Some directors, like Saless (the founder of poetic realism) in *A Simple Event* and *Still Life*, employed a realistic style; others, like Kimiavi in *The Mongols* (with its theme of the Western exploitation of Iran), *The Garden of Stone* (1975), and *P for Pelican*, used metaphoric language; and others, like Bayzaie in *Downpour* (1971), *The Journey*, *The Stranger and the Fog* (1973), and *The Crow* (1976), targeted issues of cultural identity and alienation by employing a dramatic structure and a realistic style rich with rituals.

Due to censorship during this period, the audience was prepared to read between the lines and not take anything at face value—to read everything symbolically, sometimes even in spite of the filmmaker's intention. (This still holds true today for Iranian cinema, but primarily outside the country, where there is still much mystery, stereotyping, and controversy about Iran's political system and censorship.) For example, the man with dark glasses who takes away the teacher at the end of *Downpour* was read symbolically as an agent either of fate or of the shah's secret police.

Iranian literature, culture, and language are full of multifaceted metaphors, symbols, allegories, and proverbs. This is illustrated in the traditional narrative, the magnificent *Thousand and One Nights* (mainly known in the West as *The Arabian Nights*), in which feelings, thoughts, and erotic sensations appear as animals, objects, locations, and even characters in both realistic and magical setups—what people today call magical realism—in a spiral structure of stories within stories.

Because of Iran's traditions and social conditions, Iranian culture and politics demand a covert expression of subject and self, which may on occasion result in sentimentality, romanticism, and hypocrisy. When martyrdom and selflessness are considered virtues, openness, psychologizing, and the kind of pleasure and excitement associated with pop music and the dramatic arts can be interpreted as cheap, pretentious, immoral, and self-centered—or man-centered—rather than God-centered.

Iranian religious mysticism is full of metaphors and symbols as well as allegory (as in the poetry of Rumi and Farid Ud-Din Attar), codes, and signs. It seems that due to political censorship, cultural or personal taboos, or spiritual experience, all of these in Iranian poetry, narrative, and the visual arts are inevitable whenever an incommunicable idea is being expressed. Abstraction and metaphoric language conceal meaning and talk about larger issues—as in the poems of Hafiz—for sacred purposes, secret purposes, or both. That is to say, the mysteries of the system and the universe are understood and conveyed only through metaphor.

This is why it's difficult to talk about the meaning of Paradjanov's films or some of Kiarostami's films, such as *The Wind Will Carry Us,* when one falls short of narrative justification for the esoteric nature of the films. Certain images or inspiring moments that may look insignificant or irrelevant are in fact illuminating. Moments that occur at seeming random in the middle of a scene wind up informing both the character and the viewer. In teaching Kiarostami, Bresson, and Paradjanov, I have been asked several times by my students about the meaning of their films. Forugh provides a poet's insight regarding this question: "A poet's thought enters her work like a moth behind a window or a sleeping turtle under the sun."[6]

When Iranian filmmakers apply the language and structure of poetry to their films, they arrive at a narrative that is compressed, sparse, and metaphoric. The nondramatic, minimalist, quiet, and detached poetic realism of Saless in *A Simple Event* is a perfect example. Also, like the rolling of the empty canister in *Close-up* and the apple in *The Wind Will Carry Us*, the metaphoric work in *The House Is Black* and *The Mongols*, is nonlinear—elliptical, fragmented, and associational. Similarly, the voiceovers in *The House Is Black* and *The Wind Will Carry Us* shift meanings and add to the sense of multiple realities.

The strong influence of Paradjanov's films in postrevolutionary Iran reflects the national spirit and the relevance of his symbols (carpets, clothes, ancient architecture, objects such as musical instruments, calligraphy, public baths, sacred places, and heavenly fruits such as pomegranates), entailing a system of narrative based on images, icons, and a sense of metaphysical absences and presences. This system involves a relative freedom from the structures of cause and effect and a relative absence of psychology and subjectivity that are reflected in Kiarostami's cinema. It also entails a use of shallow space in which the actors address either the camera or the offscreen space as if it were a mirror (e.g., men looking into the camera while shaving in *Report* and *The Wind Will Carry Us*), which is also the method often used for establishing a sense of depth in Persian miniatures.

A perfect example of metaphor in Kiarostami's cinema, also common in Persian poetry and the work of other Iranian filmmakers, is the use of ruins as an image of depression, an image that can be historical as well as personal—that evokes a collective memory of destruction brought about imperialistically and internally as well as a sense of despair and loss. It is a sense of alienation and longing that brings the little boy to Tehran in *The Traveler* and coaxes the heroes of *Life and Nothing More . . .*, *Taste of Cherry*, and *The Wind Will Carry Us* out of Tehran and into the country. The rubble left by the earthquake in *Life and Nothing More . . .* ("This is my studio," Kiarostami noted in a French documentary[7]) and revisited in *Through the Olive Trees* (1994); the land pulverized by bulldozers in *Taste of Cherry;* the excavation in the cemetery in *The Wind Will Carry Us;* the ruined house in the rain, damaged by war, in *A.B.C. Africa* (2001): these are the key images of ruins in Kiarostami's films. These are not only images of devastation but also sites where treasures might be found, whether these are the valuable objects retrieved from the wrecked village or the thighbone dug out of the cemetery. These images are staples of Iranian cinema and literature. They also appear in such films as Kimiavi's *P for Pelican*, Naderi's *Water, Wind, Dust* (1987), and Saless's *A Simple Event* as well as Rumi's and Hafiz's

Ruins in *A.B.C. Africa*

poetry and Omar Khayyám's *Rubáiyát.* A particularly instructive example of the imagery of ruins can be found in the works of Sadegh Hedayat,[8] the most influential writer of short fiction in twentieth-century Persian literature: his language portrays the depth of his hopelessness, isolation, and alienation with a brilliant overlay of humor and satire. His works are both philosophical and political—similar in their wrestling with existential questions of life and death to the works of Franz Kafka (whom he translated) and Fyodor Dostoyevsky, two of the most popular writers among Iranian intellectuals, especially during the 1960s and 1970s. One can find traces of Hedayat and the spirit of his work and humor in Kiarostami's films (especially *Taste of Cherry,* in which the quest of the hero recalls Hedayat's suicide at the age of forty-eight).

In *The Wind Will Carry Us,* these ruins are set against a fantasy of heaven or the promised land embodied in the village and the surrounding landscape. The ocean at the end of *Water, Wind, Dust* and the garden in the midst of a desert in *P for Pelican,* which reflect the characters' ideal destinations, can be either noticed or ignored (as in the case of Behzad) but represent longing in either case. Behzad even jokingly alludes to this when he suggests the fantasy of buried treasure as an expedient cover story. (The harmonious, heavenly village in *The Wind Will Carry Us* calls to mind the magical village in *Brigadoon* [1954]).

Since cinema is a way of thinking, symbols or metaphors, such as those in the dream sequence in *The Traveler,* are used as a form of compensation, a gesture of protest or affirmation to emphasize or exaggerate feelings or messages (in this case, the horror provoked by brutality

Ruins in *Life and Nothing More . . .* (courtesy of Mongrel Media)

against children). In *The Wind Will Carry Us,* the scenes in which the hero kicks the turtle, watches the dung beetle, or throws the thighbone into the stream all function in this manner, condensing a meaning and a character's attitude into a single image.

Thus, meaning can be communicated without being spelled out, especially for those who use poetry as a part of their conversation. (For example, in *The Wind Will Carry Us,* Behzad says, "I am addicted to my hopelessness" in reference to himself while quoting Forugh's poem to the young woman in the dark cellar.) Poetry is so popular among Iranians that many illiterate people memorize verses by Hafiz, Khayyám, and Rumi. There's a tendency among Iranian artists to adopt poetic language for their works. It's not far from the truth to say that the true culture, history, spirit, and identity of Iranians are captured in the form of poetry.

| | |

Some of this tendency to adopt poetry has been intensified by state censorship, which has played a creative role in Iranian cinema both before and since the shah's time. One constant has been a ban on providing negative images of or criticizing the government. After the Revolution, any disrespect for Islamic values and portrayals of sex and violence were forbidden. Women without proper attire or in physical contact with men and improper (i.e., "immoral") subjects such as adultery, leftism, prostitution, suicide, or Westernized values were the kinds of elements made impermissible. Parallel to this process and adding to a repressed environment was an ongoing cultural tradition of self-censorship. The creative aspect of all this grows out of the challenge presented to the filmmaker of representing ideas in codes and signs. Many ellipses in Kiarostami's work grow directly out of this process. Even his model of an interactive cinema has its roots in it.

| | |

Cinema was considered by the clergy to be a form of Western exploitation, equal to prostitution, that promoted the corruption of youth by importing Western culture to Iran. It was therefore banned by the religious leaders and angry Iranians burned more than a hundred movie theaters during the Revolution. The torching of Cinema Rex in Abadan, in which over three hundred people died while watching the Iranian film *Deers* (1975) (the perpetrator of this crime was never conclusively uncovered), was the most tragic of these fires. Following the Revolution, for a short time all the movie theaters were closed. But soon they started showing European films, including some with strong revolutionary content. In addition, films such as *State of Siege* (1973) and *The Battle of Algiers* (1965) that were banned during the shah's time were screened.

In 1982, amid all the ambiguity about cinema and its role in Iran, the Ministry of Islamic Guidance issued a set of film standards and values that banned sex and violence and any violation of Islamic and revolutionary values. The government also put a ban on Hollywood films and a partial ban on other Western films and started subsidizing films that promoted Islamic cinema. Some former filmmakers and actors were prohibited from working in film. Consequently, many first-time directors entered the scene and tried their luck. In 1983, the Farabi Cinema Foundation was established along with the Fajr Film Festival, which helped introduce and promote Iranian films to the international festivals and markets. Cinema after the Revolution had become a political, moral, and didactic issue—an apparatus that had blood on its hands and the ghost of victims on its conscience. Sometimes a film that would get permission to be screened would be pulled afterward in response to an angry clergyman or audience. At a time when the government was concerned about identity and cultural safety (Islamic and national) and their portrayal in cinema, each film was treated like a deadly weapon. There was a sense of fear and paranoid distrust as in the cold war era, when the moral values of a nation were supposed to have been under attack.

I believe it would be hard for any serious Iranian filmmaker not to think at least unconsciously about the victims of the Cinema Rex fire and be haunted by their ghosts—and thus by the whole question of Iranian cinema. Kiarostami has repeatedly addressed this issue and its role in people's lives in his films. The story of Iranian cinema is another layer hidden beneath all the other untold stories of his films. For him, cinema, as for the characters in *Close-up* and *Taste of Cherry,* is located in both heaven and hell,a place to go to learn about oneself and others through interaction. It is a cinema of meditation, devoid of the common characteristics of commercial cinema.

Close-up and *Through the Olive Trees* are about the role of cinema in people's lives. What is not possible to capture in film, one sees in the offscreen reality, as with the death of the old woman in *The Wind Will Carry Us* and the relationship between the couple in *Through the Olive Trees,* which the director only notices after the shooting is over. And what is not possible to control in real life becomes possible in one's film and creative world, as in *Taste of Cherry,* when the soldiers are no longer marching in the hills but instead are sitting casually on the film's hilly location holding flowers. In *The Wind Will Carry Us,* cinema is referred to as a medium to record death (of the old woman), which doesn't account for the unpredictability of such an adventure or the impossibility of such documenting. In *Life and Nothing More . . . ,* Kiarostami once again reminds us of the magnitude of a tragedy and the impossibility of framing it.

Case No. 1, Case No. 2, the most difficult to see of Kiarostami's features due to its banning, is also a fascinating political statement about the role of cinema at a time when its two themes, loyalty and espionage, had a great deal of resonance in Iranian society. Listening plays as important a role in this analysis as looking: the first scene features a giant ear drawn on the blackboard as part of the lesson. The film is bold and daring, though it loses some of its edge in the second half by becoming redundant.

Kiarostami films a fictional scene of a student causing a disturbance in class. A group of students is asked to leave the classroom until someone reveals the identity of the guilty student. The film has two parts: in part one, none of the students says anything to the teacher and therefore they all are kept outside the classroom. In part two, one student reveals the identity of the guilty party and therefore is allowed to reenter the class. Kiarostami shows this fictional film (or at least implies that he shows it) to a number of parents as well as cultural and political figures. Some support the solidarity of the students in not revealing the secret. Others support the behavior of the student who informs the teacher about the guilty party. There are also times when he shows people talking about the hypothetical situation in relative terms. (They say that if the loyalty or espionage is beneficial to the society, it's justifiable; otherwise, it's wrong.) Throughout this analysis, he alludes to cinema by showing certain relevant objects—a film spool, a roll of film, a projector—as an integral part of his own film's design, either as parts of individual compositions or in separate shots. This is a procedure he would subsequently adapt in *Homework*, using the same principle in reverse by focusing on the children instead of the authorities.

Kiarostami might well have asked his interview subjects, Do you think cinema should show reality—tell the truth—or not, and if it does, should it be penalized? Which decision is morally right for the educational system as well as the children? It's worth noting that Sedegh Ghotbzadeh, the head of state television who is interviewed in the film, established TV censorship in Iran; a year or so later, he was executed for committing espionage for the CIA.

| | |

Kiarostami is often present in his films as a part of the reality he is filming, whether he's onscreen or off-screen. At the beginning of *Homework* we hear him explaining what the film is about to a curious passerby. Later, in several parts of the film, we see him and his camera filming the children and also possibly frightening some of them. In *Orderly or Disorderly* (1981), we hear him talking to his camera crew about the length of time required for the kids to get on or off the bus and about his own interests while filming the shot. Apparently, in a school he has more control in creating a sense of order or disorder than on the street, where neither he nor a policeman is able to control the traffic in an orderly manner.

In *Close-Up,* too, he puts in appearances both offscreen and on-screen. Initially we hear him inquiring offscreen about Sabzian's whereabouts in the police station; later we see him on-screen when he visits Sabzian in prison. On other occasions we hear him speaking to the Ahankhah family, to the judge in the courtroom, and, during the final sequence, to his camera crew while they follow Makhmalbaf and his double. In all these situations, we are reminded that he's filming and become aware of the filmmaker's power, both as a judge and as someone who intervenes in reality.

In *Life and Nothing More . . . , Through the Olive Trees,* and *The Wind Will Carry Us,* Kiarostami uses actors to stand in for him (though he also makes a very brief, almost accidental appearance in the second of these films, when the film crew is shooting several takes of a scene). Furthermore, the whole subject of *Through the Olive Trees* is directing villagers (on the set and in life) in a remote village—just as *Life and Nothing More . . .* is about having made a film in a remote village. In the final scene of *Through the Olive Trees,* the director figure, turning from the film to "life and nothing more," persuades Hossein to walk after Tahereh rather than ride on the truck and then follows him for a bit to see how far he goes. Kiarostami appears again in the flesh at the end of *Taste of Cherry,* again with his own crew, and again throughout *A.B.C. Africa,* which is structured around his trip to Uganda, his presence there, and his interactions with Ugandans. His impressions come to the fore during a lengthy conversation with his assistant in the dark, and this scene evokes a sense of reality in Africa that otherwise would have been impossible to capture. (Full darkness comes after electricity is shut off at night.) Like the darkness at the end of the grave scene in *Taste of Cherry,* this darkness creates an intimate space in which the audience can share an experience; in *A.B.C. Africa,* it also makes the audience directly aware of Kiarostami's presence.

Most of these appearances and self-representations are implicitly or explicitly forms of self-criticism that include criticism of media as well as class. The character shown is typically a middle-aged, middle-class urban intellectual man, sometimes unsympathetic (*Taste of Cherry, The*

Wind Will Carry Us), whose profession, as Chris Marker once wrote in praise of Forugh's understanding of despair, is hopelessness.[9] This self-criticism makes his films not only political but also personal.

The inclusion of himself as part of the reality he is filming at times has negative connotations. In self-defense, Sabzian in prison asks Kiarostami if he thinks being a filmmaker makes him a swindler like himself. Some of these negative connotations suggest a relatively innocent swindler, as in *The Traveler* and *Close-up*, while some suggest more blatant deception, as in *Taste of Cherry* and *The Wind Will Carry Us*. (In *Through the Olive Trees*, he's somewhere in between.)

But who is the real swindler: the filmmaker (Kiarostami)? the audience who has paid to sit in the dark to watch the film? the family in *Close-up* who willingly went along with the charade? or the poor, unemployed print shop worker, Sabzian, who, in need of expressing himself, attained a temporary status of power and respect, for which he is punished because he belongs to the working class?

"Lies carry a kind of truth," Kiarostami said in one of his interviews.[10] Some of the people in Kiarostami's films who lie include the children in *Homework* (when they say they prefer doing homework to watching cartoons), Sabzian, the family he fools, Behzad (about the buried treasure), and Kiarostami himself.

To what extent are Kiarostami's films apolitical? It all depends on what we mean by political. For instance, we might say that there is political significance in that in most of Kiarostami's films—especially *Close-up*, *Taste of Cherry*, and *The Wind Will Carry Us*—the characters are defined through their jobs. Kiarostami himself says it. In an unpublished February 2000 interview in Tehran, I asked him about the political position of his films—in particular *The Wind Will Carry Us*, which I thought was his most political film—and the importance of characters' jobs in defining them. He replied, "As soon as you have a job you become political. There are two kinds of apolitical films: either they have no identity or they insist that they are political, as in the case of party films, where appearances and belonging to a particular class clearly defend a particular ideology. For example, [when] talking about the oppression of the master, the job of the master and the job of the peasant aren't known and their relationships are not clear either, because one takes the side of the peasants in any case."

In *Close-up*, there is a great deal of emphasis on Sabzian's unemployment and on the fact that the Ahankhah sons have not been able to find the jobs they've been trained for. When Mehrdad talks about his brother's unemployment and mentions that he works in a bread company, his mother, in Turkish, asks him to be quiet. Incidentally, this suggests that Kiarostami may not always understand what they're saying and that unemployment and menial work are a disgrace for the well-to-do, not merely the poor (which perhaps explains why cinema is as glamorous to them as it is to Sabzian).

In *Taste of Cherry*, every character is understood through his job except for the hero (and even he, at the end, is revealed as an actor): the plastic garbage collector (my personal favorite), the Afghan seminary student, the Kurdish soldier, and the Turkish taxidermist. The same is true in *The Wind Will Carry Us*. "When we meet people in a friendly gathering," Kiarostami added during our conversation in Tehran, "right away we want to know what they do. But in cinema it's been accepted that the identity of character is not necessary—they are supposed to entertain you. Most characters in films have no neighborhood, no jobs, we don't know what kind of family relationships they have. But if the film wants to take a deeper look at a character, we have to do it."

The problem with many political films is that they focus only on external conditions and outside pressures, leaving out cultural, traditional, and personal elements. With his philosophical views and humor, Kiarostami points to the inner worlds of his characters—the anger and despair of Mr. Badii, the turmoil of Behzad—that are usually out of reach except through dramatization or metaphors. In *The Wind Will Carry Us*, Behzad, who is waiting for the death of the old woman, speaks to an offscreen man who throws up a thighbone while digging a hole for a telecommunications post, thereby echoing the hero's preoccupation with death. Behzad eventually throws away the bone, which he has kept in his car throughout the film, and as an ending this is significant because it shows a shift in his attitude.

Likewise, it seems significant that in *Taste of Cherry*, when Badii lingers at a dusty construction site—perhaps to contemplate what it means to be buried—he's asked to move by a construction worker. This interaction suggests that his fantasy of hell is the reality of the construction worker's job. Badii becomes both the agent to inform us about these marginal, multicultural people and a slightly distorted reflection of them. Similarly, the boy in *The Wind Will Carry Us* represents an innocence that Behzad once had and perhaps craves to have again. Behzad is the embodiment of the universal, modern, alienated, anxious, and preoccupied man. By introducing alienation in the East, Kiarostami breaks a stereotype of the Western world about Iran (many Westerners regard alienation strictly as a Western phenomenon and as a product of advanced industrial capitalism).

In Kiarostami's later films, the presence or absence of women and their treatment are probably not as dramatic as they are in *Report,* but they are far more characteristic.[11] The absence of women begins in his prerevolutionary commercials: out of the first 150 that he made between 1960 and 1969, the first 50 had no women at all. This pattern of avoidance continues all the way through *Taste of Cherry,* though the reasons for it vary according to the period. Before the Revolution, Kiarostami might have been resisting the exploitation of women in advertising. But after the Revolution he had censorship to worry about, because any portrayal of an intimate relationship between a man and woman would violate the Islamic codes, a taboo that imparted a certain artificiality to films. Kiarostami couldn't show women indoors without their head scarves, which may account for why he tended to avoid interiors altogether.

By itself, the idea of absent women is not so significant, except in reference to the censorship that limits the situations in which women can be portrayed in film. (Ironically, affectionate touching was forbidden but aggressive assaults were tolerated.) The absence could be read as a rejection on Kiarostami's part—a decision not to dedicate screen time to women characters. But what is interesting is that often in his films, absences strongly suggest presences. For example, the absent women in *Taste of Cherry*—which many viewers interpret as the source of the hero's romantic despair—and in most of Kiarostami's short films, especially the absent urban women in *Life and Nothing More . . .* and *The Wind Will Carry Us,* could indicate another part of the hero's life that is absent or missing. The rural women in his films, other than the anthropological characters, suggest an ideal woman who is innocent, strong, and in tune with nature. Some common representations found in Iranian cinema generally, not only in Kiarostami's films, are of idealized rural women, particularly the shy young women washing dishes or clothes in *Life and Nothing More . . .* or auditioning in *Through the Olive Trees* and the woman washing clothes the day after the birth of her child in *The Wind Will Carry Us.* In *Through the Olive Trees,* the provocative images of omnipresent schoolgirls in black lead to the single image of Tahereh, who never becomes a character. Throughout the film she is treated as a desired woman, quiet and mysterious, like the middle-class girl who rejects the boy in *The Experience* (1973) (or the fantasy movie star in the same film's shooting game), not to mention the young milkmaid in *The Wind Will Carry Us.*

Idealized women in postrevolutionary Iranian cinema have ranged from mothers (of the martyrs) and wives (of the heroes) to little girls and teenagers. In *Baran* (2001), Majid Majidi's most recent film, the ideal woman is a little Afghan girl who does not speak a word. The roles of women in more recent films have ranged from rebellious teenagers or students to prostitutes or domesticated, subservient wives (as portrayed in Mehrjui's films)—all of them a far cry from Kiarostami's complex characters. But women as either victims or providers haven't shown much complexity except in works by Bayzaie and Bani-Etemad. The mother in *Where Is the Friend's House?* is preoccupied, insensitive, and aggressive to her son except for when she feeds him; she exploits him to take care of the baby, buy bread, and perform other household chores. And the mother in *The Traveler* is incapable of disciplining her child and consequently submits him to a beating by his schoolmaster—she asks him to punish the boy for stealing money and lying so that he learns the lesson of good behavior and moral values.

The century-old dying woman in *The Wind Will Carry Us* is interfering with the hero's work—she is an invisible character who overshadows the whole film. The hero's wife and his female boss, both of whom are on the phone with him from Tehran, control him from a distance. And in the cellar he cites the poetry of Forugh, the film's most important invisible woman, to the milkmaid in a mechanical way, knowing that she may not know the poet or even understand what he is talking about. All these invisible women are related to death or absence: Forugh died young in an accident, the poem that the milkmaid listens to is about death, his boss speaks to him about the dying woman, and his wife speaks to him about a family funeral that she wants him to attend. Both con-

The schoolmaster and a boy in *The Traveler*

versations take place in the cemetery. Similarly, in *Through the Olive Trees,* Hossein meets and falls in love with Tahereh in a cemetery.

Kiarostami's progressive and demanding women start to emerge in *Case No. 1, Case No. 2,* in which two educated professional women give their opinions about the issues of education and disciplining children. The little girls in *The Chorus* (1982) learn to unite and together call the hard-of-hearing grandfather—a recurring figure from *Bread and Alley* (1970)—to open the door. *The Wind Will Carry Us* is a leap in its inclusion of a group of strong women, starting with the woman who serves tea in the village coffee shop. When the hero says that he is amazed to see her, not a man, serve tea, she responds humorously, "Didn't your mother ever serve tea to your father? Then don't say you haven't seen one." In other scenes she challenges a village man who thinks that his job is more tiring than hers.

A.B.C. Africa is filled with children and strong women. One woman, caught in the panning of the camera while Kiarostami films an outdoor class, gracefully passes by, ignoring the camera; another woman sits in the street speaking in Persian, saying, "You trickster, you're back, I know you love me"; and other women, such as the manager of the AIDS organization, are interviewed.

Unlike many who hold the absence of women in Kiarostami's films as a strike against him, I don't believe that every filmmaker should talk about every important issue. They're not responsible for expressing all that is lacking in cinema or in reality. They cannot talk for all the repressed and all the deprived. Filmmakers should be committed to conveying the truth that they are aware of or have experienced and should be judged based on what they put on the screen. My only objection to Kiarostami in regard to women is to their depiction in *Report,* in which his camera is less sensitive toward the wife than it is toward the children who are abused in his other films. We are with the husband all the time.

In the copy of *Report* that is available now—in addition to being banned, probably due to the woman's uncovered hair and lack of proper attire—a picture of the shah in all the shots in the government office has been scratched out. (Shortly after the Revolution, the women improperly shown in such films as Roberto Rossellini's *Open City* [1945] were similarly scratched out.) According to Bahman Farmanara, the film's producer, a scene with a prostitute is missing—a scene that according to him made the hero feel guilty and thus motivated his subsequent wife beating. I have no memory of this scene, but I vividly recall a sex scene between the couple, also missing, in which the husband's behavior is mechanical and selfish and the wife chatters the whole time about money. Her awfulness throughout almost desensitizes us to his hostile behavior toward her later on. To Kiarostami's credit, he films the blows through a half-open door so he does not show us the full scene of violence when the husband beats the wife.[12] As Kiarostami said in an interview when the film was first screened, the crew was upset and crying while watching the domestic scenes being shot. They were too real.[13]

The unexpected long scene in the deli adds liveliness to the film; every man there is talking about cars, symbols of class (the hero does not have a car). Except for *Solution* (1978), which I will discuss later, cars are a significant element in Kiarostami's films starting with this one, in which the hero drives to a shopping district, a deli, and a hospital. His car doesn't run properly, and he gets into a frustrating traffic jam that winds up partially motivating his anger toward his wife. The same preoccupation with cars continues through *A.B.C. Africa.*

Traffic has always been a problem in Tehran, but following the Revolution and a few years into the war, traffic became worse with many used and old cars in the streets, partly due to the population explosion and the immigration of many people to Tehran. The volume of traffic has increased to unhealthy levels, physically and mentally.

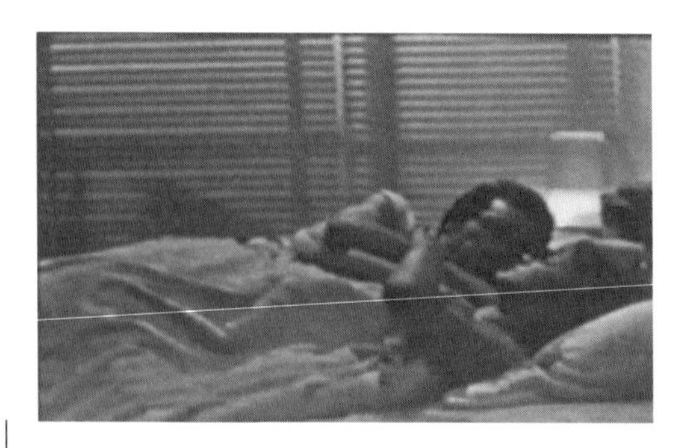

The husband and the wife in *Report*

In Kiarostami's films there is an identification of the car with the hero that relates to both class and personality. In the final sequence of *Life and Nothing More* . . . the hero's car, seen in extreme long shot, represents the character. Earlier in the film, when he uses his car to block certain roads in ruined villages, he's posing an obstruction to the villagers. In *Orderly or Disorderly,* especially the last sequence, the behavior of people in their cars, seen from a high angle, is a strong indication of their social nature.

The car in modern life has become the ultimate private and sacred space for individuals who spend a good portion of their lives behind wheels. They do business, drive, eat, and meditate on the road, among other activities, and their cars constitute a kind of personal armor. (Significantly, when Badii in *Taste of Cherry* finally decides to kill himself, he leaves his car behind and takes a cab. And before Bezhad throws away the thighbone in *The Wind Will Carry Us,* he rinses off his windshield.)

The tire in *Solution* that the hero needs for his car reveals a very ironic relationship between man and machine, a kind of mutual dependence. Although he rolls the tire down a hill, several close-ups of the tire in motion make it seem autonomous, with a will of its own, as in Rumi's poem #322:

> You are my polo ball,
> running before the stick of my command
> I am always running along after you,
> though it is I who make you move.[14]

Another significant political and ethical theme in most of Kiarostami's films is the issue of child exploitation, as in *Recess, The Experience, The Traveler, The Wedding Suit, Where Is the Friend's House?* and *Homework. The Traveler* shows the beating of the young boy by his schoolmaster, at the request of his own mother, who is unable to discipline him. *Recess* shows the beating of a child for breaking a window, though the only evidence we have that he's guilty comes in a printed title—one integrated in the composition in a way that reflects Kiarostami's background in design and credit sequences. *The Wedding Suit* unveils the exploitation of children at work as well as a beating of one of them, which we also see in *The Experience.*

Finally, the violence toward children in all these films culminates in the powerful and heartbreaking *Homework,* in which we witness stories of children's physical punishment, at times with a belt, by their parents and other adults. *Homework,* in a simple but extremely focused style, exhibits the little tortured souls who belong to a museum of torture—the contemporary Iranian classroom. As they are asked to stand in front of the camera to tell their stories, often against their will, they become the prisoners of the educational system (both in school and at home) as well as the film frame—and another level of anxiety is introduced to their experiences. The film suggests the potential consequences of such humiliation, violence, and horror and the future these children are looking forward to. In fact, one of the boys even talks about killing Saddam Hussein when he grows up. Kiarostami reminds him that Hussein might not be there when he's grown up, but the child insists on his desire. Another monumental addition to the film is the question of war, including religious martyrdom and the preparation of the young generation for the enemy. One can conclude that both the beatings of the children and their training to become warriors are their real homework and the goal of their education. The suffering, pain, fear of authorities, and anxiety of the children while telling their stories—which are only understood by their friends—are unfortunate. It is significant that *Homework* is filmed in a poor public school in Tehran and that the parents of the children are mostly illiterate and poor. (Teachers used to beat children at school in Iran, as in many other places—a practice that has now mainly been abandoned.) As in *Life and Nothing More . . . ,* the film reflects larger issues about war and training for war. And Kiarostami's elimina-

The opening title in *Recess*

tion of the soundtrack during the religious revolutionary chanting makes us notice the true nature of children at play.

Kiarostami clearly takes the side of the children in *Homework*. He uses methods of distancing both when he uses reverse-angle shots of himself and when he cuts the children's sounds when they are chanting. He uses cinema in *Homework* to discipline the viewers' minds in terms of the issues presented to them. (In *A.B.C. Africa,* he turns to the question of white parents adopting an African baby, and the potential consequences for the baby of such cultural displacement are in a way as important as being orphaned or dying from AIDS.)

One virtue of Kiarostami's films, implicit in the examples explored above, is their breaking of stereotypes and expectations. None of his characters is only two-dimensional. His characters, like Dostoyevsky's, have many sides and are full of conflicts. They are both the saviors and the criminals—modern and traditional, innocent and guilty. The mother in *The Traveler* who submits her child to the schoolmaster for physical punishment is as innocent (and as guilty) as the boy who is punished, who cheats both her and his friends to go to Tehran. The boy in *The Wedding Suit* who bullies the other boy into getting the suit is an unpleasant victim. In *Orderly or Disorderly* and *Fellow Citizen* (1983), the people who suffer from bad traffic are also creating it. I don't know of another Iranian director whose heroes are both innocent and corrupt.

This dualism in Kiarostami's characters is evident in *Orderly or Dis-*

orderly, one of Kiarostami's most artistic works, in which the idea of order is analyzed from different perspectives with graphic sensibility and humor. Order is portrayed as straight lines and disorder as zigzag or broken lines—the two possibilities of social behavior for both children and adults.

If children resist discipline as a part of their playful nature, adults rebel against traffic signs as a symbol of their disrespect and dissatisfaction about the imposed order of a system that is indifferent to them. This social behavior reveals chaos and the difficulty of controlling populated areas where there's a lack of civilized behavior. In fact, Kiarostami, in a short story entitled "A Good, Good Citizen," makes a point of noticing the respect of a homeless woman for traffic signs—a woman who is obviously ignored by her society. She has lost everything except her respect for traffic signs.[15]

Orderly or Disorderly not only shows the conflict of order between individuals and society but also underlines the conflict of order between the filmmaker and his subject. The form of the film as the kind of order that the filmmaker (especially the documentarian) wants to impose on his subject is at odds with the disorder of his subject. The students and drivers are beyond the control of the filmmaker. The traffic officer who eventually leaves the scene at the end of the film is a good indication of this chaos. Kiarostami's failure to capture his (theoretical) last shot of orderly traffic is his most hilarious and philosophical statement about documentary filmmaking. But, understanding the role of order in speeding the mass movements, the audience can imagine the scene that he can't capture. The film moves from perfect control toward complete chaos.

Orderly or Disorderly is a good example of a film that is free from literature, theater, or any narrative structure. Its meaning and humor are derived mainly from its cinematic form, that is, long shots and the voiceover of Kiarostami speaking to his camera crew, which plays a key role in creating a sense of expectation and humor. Similar to the use of slates at the beginning of each shot, Kiarostami's voice brings us close to the subject and at the same time keeps us distant from it.

Kiarostami's failure to shoot the orderly scene at the end of *Orderly or Disorderly* is echoed in *The Wind Will Carry Us*. Behzad and his crew cannot shoot the death ceremony of the old woman, for which they have come to the village. Here, the order of nature (death) and its unpredictability not only creates a sense of morbid humor but also helps Behzad come to some kind of self-realization and give up his original plan. Once again, the audience can imagine what Kiarostami is unable to shoot. (Interestingly enough, the film went through three title changes that reflect both Kiarostami's own gradual change of emphasis and the evolution of his hero: from *Special Ceremony* to *Eclipse* to *Journey to Morning* and then eventually to *The Wind Will Carry Us*.)

Kiarostami focuses again on the traffic and the disrespectful behavior of Tehran drivers in *Fellow Citizen*—this time with less artistic vigor (especially in the music at the end, which seems redundant). Working again with the theme of a failed mission, he reveals the attitudes of both the officer and the drivers toward traffic regulations and how arbitrary they can be. The officer, standing in front of a blocked street and listening to every story and excuse, lets some drivers in while stopping the others, his decisions based entirely on his personal judgment. Here, there's an inconsistency of social discipline on both sides of the law in which tribalism and favoritism play typical roles.

In *Taste of Cherry,* Kiarostami again plays with the idea of order and the director's control, in terms of both film (fiction) and video (documentary). If the fictional part of the film ends with Badii lying in the grave, submitting himself to death and despair, the documentary sequence shot on video shows another possibility of order, which is more liberating and reflects Kiarostami's freedom to create as he instructs his army of extras and crew. The most important thing may be that neither possibility is conclusive—significantly, a brief sequence in total darkness separates the two—because the meaning is ultimately left to the viewer.

This latter tendency culminates in the seven-minute sequence in the darkness in *A.B.C. Africa,* in which Kiarostami's taste for ellipses is combined with the same kind of ambiguity expressed in his long shots, even when they impose a moral discipline by establishing distance. But here as well, creativity—his own joined with ours—winds up playing a role; the lighting of matches and the bursts of lightning and thunder that ultimately lead us out of the darkness are the essence of his art, flashes of illumination in the midst of total uncertainty.

Notes

1. Mehrnaz Saeed-Vafa, "Bresson, Naghash-i ke ba Cinemayash Sher Migouyad" (Bresson, a painter who writers poetry with his images), *Cinema Haft* 35 (May–July 1978): 5–21.

2. See Kiarostami's testimony in Jean-Pierre Limosin, *Abbas Kiarostami: Vérités et mensonges,* in *Cinéma de notre temps* (AMIP, La Sept Arte, INA, 1994, SECAM video).

3. Sohrab Sepehry, "Address," *The Expanse of Green: Poems of Sohrab Sepehry,* trans. David L. Martin (Los Angeles: Kalimat Press/UNESCO, 1988), 45–46.

4. Forugh Farrokhzad, "Green Illusion," *Remembering the Flight: Twenty Poems by Forugh Farrokhzad,* trans. Ahmad Karimi-Hakkak (Port Coquitlam, Canada: Nik Publishers, 1997), 55.

5. Maulana Jalal al-Din Rumi, *A Garden beyond Paradise: The Mystical Poetry of Rumi,* trans. Jonathan Star and Shahram Shiva (New York: Bantam Books, 1992), 54.

6. Forugh Farrokhzad, *Bargozide-ye Ashar-e Forugh Farrokhzad* (A selection of the poems of Forugh Farrokhzad), 5th ed. (Tehran: Sherkat-e Sahami-ye Ketabha-ye Jibi, 1977), 10.

7. Limosin, *Abbas Kiarostami.*

8. The only book by Sedagh Hedayat (sometimes spelled Hidayat) in English that is currently in print is *The Blind Owl,* trans. D. P. Costello (New York: Grove Press, 1989). See also *The Blind Owl and Other Hedayat Stories,* comp. Carol L. Sayers, ed. Russell P. Christensen (Minneapolis: Sorayya Publishers, 1984), and Hassan Kamshad's *Modern Persian Prose Literature* (Bethesda, Md.: Iranbooks, 1996), 137–208. For further information see Farzin Yazdanfar's Web site devoted to Hedayat, <http://www.geocities.com/paris/tower/2943/index.html>.

9. Chris Marker, "Salgard-e Forugh Farrokhzad" (The anniversary of Forugh Farrokhzad) *Talash* 8 (Feb. 1967): 16. See also Gholam Haydari, *Forugh Farrokhzad Va Sinema* (Forugh Farrokhzad and cinema) (Tehran: Nashr-e Elm, 1998), 405–6.

10. Majid Islami, Houshang Golmakani, and Iran Karimi, "A Group Interview with Kiarostami: Goal: An Eliminating of Directing," *Film Monthly* (Tehran) 12.168: 121.

11. In Kiarostami's fifty-two-second contribution to *Lumière and Company* (see filmography), we see a close-up of two eggs frying and hear the voice of a woman, apparently coming from an answering machine, who invites a man to dinner. The cooking of this archetypal food by a single man can be read as a rejection of the woman's invitation.

12. There is a scene in the middle of the film in which the hero looks directly into the camera as if it were a mirror and cleans his face—it is almost identical to a shot in *The Wind Will Carry Us.* This direct address of the viewer can be

read as a way of reminding the audience that they are watching their own reality on the screen, that he is one of them.

13. Jamal Omid, *Tarikh-e Cinema-ye Iran* (History of Iranian cinema) (Tehran: Entesharat-e Rozaneh, 1995), 740.

14. Maulana Jalal al-Din Rumi, #322, *Kolliyat-e Shams* (Collected poems), ed. Badi Al-Zaman Faruzanfar (Tehran: Tehran University Press, 1967). This poem was translated into English expressly for this study by Franklin D. Lewis.

15. Abbas Kiarostami, "A Good, Good Citizen," trans. Minou Moshiri, *Film International* 3.2 (Spring 1995): 54–61.

A Dialogue between the Authors

September 3, 2001, Chicago

JONATHAN ROSENBAUM: You were the one who originally had the idea that we do this book together. And maybe we should both consider why we thought it was a good idea.

MEHRNAZ SAEED-VAFA: Basically, as far as I remember, we had a lot of interesting dialogues about Iranian cinema and Kiarostami, and I thought it would be a great idea to put our effort into a book. We started our dialogue in 1992, at a time when Kiarostami was getting discovered in France but still unknown in the United States. And I respected you highly as a critic and I knew that you were respected among other readers outside the United States as well as inside. Part of me really wanted you to get interested in this cinema so that you would write about it. I knew that if I spoke about how great either Kiarostami or some other Iranian filmmakers were, no one would believe me. They would say, "Oh, she's Iranian and she wants to promote her own culture here." But if *you* spoke about it no one would say that. By the same token, if you spoke highly of Kiarostami or Iranian cinema, Iranians in Iran would trust you more than me, because if I did that they'd say, "She's one of us." And then, much later, I thought it would be interesting to compare how you see him and I see him and to put that in a book for other people to see how both of us, coming from different backgrounds—

JR: I think the difference between our backgrounds is important—a Jewish American man and an Islamic Iranian woman—despite the fact that our tastes in film tend to be similar. We even had a little bit of the same formation as filmgoers insofar as we were both living in London in the mid-1970s, well over a decade before we first met in Chicago. One thing that also occurs to me is that, in a funny sort of way, both Americans and Iranians are very deprived in their access to information about cinema. In Iran, this is largely due to censorship and because of the way everything is conveyed by gossip—most often very unreliable gossip. And in this country, paradoxically, where the big companies tend to rule the discourse we have about movies, we haven't had any images at all of Iran except for what we've started to get in relation to Iranian films.

Even in that area, there's a lot of hearsay and guesswork that's going on constantly, sometimes making the most basic information hard to access.[1] Do you remember how we both spent months trying to determine whether or not *The Wind Will Carry Us* [1999] was banned in Iran—and, if so, what the censors' objections were? Then we both went to the Fajr Film Festival early this year [2001] and were told that the only reason why it hadn't opened in Iran was that it was decided that the film wouldn't make much money! Of course, the fact that Iranian censors aren't obliged to give any explanations affects this overall lack of information. In any case, considering the somewhat different contacts and resources we both have, it seemed that if we pooled these things, perhaps we could both learn more.

MS: The physical distance between the two countries is of course reduced now with the Internet. But because of all the years of political hostility between these countries, there's not much exchange, especially from the side of America. I think Iranians know more about Americans than Americans know about Iranians. We were brought up with American culture, Western culture.

JR: I remember you telling me about the Dean Martin and Jerry

Lewis movies you saw in Tehran as a child, which really surprised me at the time.

MS: There's even an interesting link one could make between *Orderly or Disorderly* [1981] and *The Disorderly Orderly* [1964]—a Jerry Lewis film directed by Frank Tashlin—quite apart from the similarity of the English titles. But the chaos in Lewis's film is internalized, whereas in Kiarostami's film it's completely externalized.

I had also seen major American cities before coming here, in a lot of documentaries and feature films. I had a very good idea of where I was coming to. But even a critic like you who reads a lot and travels a lot—you still have ideas about Iran that are based on a lack of proper information.

JR: I'm sure that must be true. I was quite startled, for instance, when I learned that 65 percent of the current Iranian population is under twenty-five—and even more taken aback when I learned that the ages when you can vote and get married in Iran are much younger than they are in Western countries. This suggests that the paradigms we use for understanding Iran are often faulty to begin with. Could you provide me with any other examples?

MS: Well, I frequently encounter in a lot of Americans a confusion between the political identity and the traditional identity of Iranians. It's also questionable how much you can actually learn about a given culture through films—which applies to Iranians understanding Americans as well as vice versa. The biggest problem is the absence of a context for new information. For example, the issue of suicide in *Taste of Cherry* [1997] being Islamically incorrect was allowed to overshadow almost everything else that was said in the United States about the film.

JR: We should acknowledge that our viewpoints about Kiarostami differ in terms of what kind of information we consider most important. For me, Kiarostami is first of all a global filmmaker and secondarily an Iranian filmmaker. For you, he's first of all an Iranian filmmaker. Even though I'm interested in learning about Iran through Iranian cinema, and his films are certainly a part of that, I feel that I go to his films to learn about the world, not just Iran. There are surely other Iranian filmmakers who could tell me more about Iran than he can, but I don't think that there are any other Iranian filmmakers now who could tell me as much about the world in general.

MS: How do you mean? Cinematically or politically or . . . ?

JR: I compare him to Jean-Luc Godard in the 1960s—the time extending from, say, *The Married Woman* to *Weekend:* only a stretch of about three years, 1964 to 1967, though it encompasses eight features and several shorts. If you wanted to know what was going on in the Western world at that time, you'd go to his movies—because he had this capacity to pick up on all these things that were current in the culture, and it wasn't necessarily because he was seeking this. It was just because he was sufficiently open to it in terms of his interests—and I guess it *is* significant that Godard was one of the first to pick up on Kiarostami's importance. (He once told me how he stayed over in Paris a few extra days on one of his trips from Switzerland in order to see more of his films.)

Godard was reflecting what was going on through the culture of cities—and I think that in the 1960s, to know what was going on in the world, cities were very important. Today, I suspect that the country, the suburbs, and the sticks are more important. The reason why is that the whole world is united now by what the large multinational companies are doing everywhere, and you can see more of what they're doing in the country than you can in the city. The mobile phone in *The Wind Will Carry Us* is a perfect example. Or you might recall that when this film finally opened in Chicago, this was at the same time they were doing those recounts of the votes during the presidential election. And I wrote in the *Chicago Reader* that the film was actually speaking to this [December 8, 2000]. How? Because there's an enormous rift now between what's happening in the media and what's happening in everyday life—a rift that gets expressed through one's perception of time, one's body language, and all sorts of other things. If you turned to someone on the street during that postelection period, you could immediately bond with them about what was going on, but if you turned on the TV, all you'd encounter was people screaming at one another. It was a different reality. This kind of discrepancy is captured perfectly in *The Wind Will Carry Us,* which shows such a division quite comically. So it shouldn't be so surprising that what he's doing is appreciated and recognized as relevant by people across the world.

MS: Yeah. They see something in *The Wind Will Carry Us,* and although the hero is a man, I can see my own reflection in him. I'm like him too, driven by anxiety to do lots of stuff and be preoccupied, not be there—you know, as I put it in my essay [in this volume], he's an image of modern man.

JR: Yes, and of course we're media people, too. You know, maybe the fact that Kiarostami is so contemporary is what makes him so controversial.

MS: Do you mean controversial inside Iran or outside?

JR: Both. But what I'm mainly thinking about now is how some of my colleagues—including one critic in Buenos Aires and another one in Melbourne, among others—really dislike *A.B.C. Africa* [2001], and I'm not even sure why. It's also just been rejected by the New York Film Festival. I can certainly agree with the point you made to Kiarostami in Tehran, when we saw the film in rough cut—that it should have been called *A.B.C. Uganda* and not *A.B.C. Africa*. (Also, more trivially, there's a typo in the title card for some reason—"*A.B.C*" *Africa*, without the final period.) But otherwise it seems to me a perfectly respectable minor work that responsibly fulfills its own (admittedly modest) social agenda, and I find the whole latter section—basically everything from the visit to the hospital onward—quite powerful. So I'm not clear at this point what the real objections are—unless it's a disapproval of him showing so many kids dancing or maybe just of him making a film outside Iran. They say it's lazy, for one thing—

MS: I'm not sure what they mean by lazy, either—but if they're right, that's a virtue, not a vice.

JR: What do you mean?

MS: One sign of mastery is for the work to look extremely simple, as if anyone can do it. Think of [Charlie] Chaplin's direction, which looks like he simply found his shots rather than worked hard to find them. The arrangement of shots in *A.B.C. Africa* and the overall rhythm are really musical, but some people don't notice this.

JR: We know that he worked on the editing a long time, partly because he hadn't edited digital video before. I can remember when we saw it for the first time that it didn't look so much like a Kiarostami film during the first half—maybe because the exposition and interviews seemed relatively conventional.

MS: But isn't this information important to the film?

JR: Of course it is.

MS: This is the first Kiarostami film in which the subject might be said to overwhelm the treatment of it—which maybe creates a conflict in some people's minds.

JR: Yes—which is often a conflict between what's artful and what's socially useful.

MS: But what did they expect from Kiarostami, anyway, knowing his style?

JR: Maybe the fact that so much is expected from him these days is partially to blame. Do you think that expectations of this kind are partly behind the hostility toward his work in Iran, despite the fact that he's been such a major influence there?

MS: I don't believe there's hostility against him—just a certain kind of criticism. Some think he's overrated, but they're not ruling him out. And of course his last two films haven't even opened there commercially yet.

The fact that he's won so many prizes in festivals is partly why his cinema has been so influential, especially for younger filmmakers—who in fact often do get prizes of their own when they follow his lead.

JR: Part of the problem is that he tends to be either deified or demonized. For the same reason, some people may place too much value on his still photography or his poetry. I happen to like the former much more than the latter, maybe because it seems more directly relevant to his films.

MS: I agree, although I like the rhythm of his poetry and the atmosphere of some of his landscapes. But it's only in his cinema that these things become truly meaningful. The same thing applies to [Sergei] Paradjanov's collages and paintings.

JR: Another example I can give for Kiarostami's global relevance at least as far back as *Close-up* [1990] is the striking and interesting similarity between that film and the story of John Guare's play *Six Degrees of Separation,* which surfaced somewhat later and which [in 1993] became a film as well. That was also based on a true story. A young black man befriended a very well-to-do New York couple, claiming to be the son of Sidney Poitier and offering to get them involved in a Broadway show that he claimed his father was putting on. He got invited to be the couple's house guest, and it was some time before his fraud was uncovered. The fact that something so similar could happen in New York and Tehran fascinates me, though some of the differences are also important, such as the issue of race in the Guare play. Yet as you point out in your essay, the issue of ethnicity, which some Westerners may not notice—the fact that Sabzian happens to be Turkish—plays a significant role in *Close-up*. (In fact, the multiculturalism of Kiarostami's films is another "global" aspect of them.) I remember you were saying back in 1992, when I saw the film for the first time in Toronto, that the kind of respect that cinema has in Iran immediately gives a kind of empowerment to people who are filmmakers. Ordinary people defer to them, and that becomes a very interesting subject in itself; in fact, every film Kiarostami has made since then relates to this theme in one way or another.

MS: It's interesting. When I was a teenager, everyone was a poet, but now everyone is a filmmaker, especially after the Revolution. Seeing that [*Close-up*] for the first time, so many [Iranian] filmmakers were not educated in film—and many were not educated, period. But becoming a filmmaker or artist originally conferred a status that was reserved only for the privileged or the educated and then, all of a sudden, it became something noneducated people could achieve, if they worked hard to get there.

JR: Yes, and [Mohsen] Makhmalbaf became the role model for that, as *Close-up* shows. You compare the function of cinema in Iran to that of basketball for black youth in the United States [see the essay in this volume], which is also quite suggestive. It's a ticket to class mobility—you might even describe it as a way to get out of town, if you live in a suburb or a village.

MS: Well, that's changed now. In Iran it's no longer such a big deal to make a film. Kiarostami has raised the bar, so that now you have to win a prize in a major film festival, preferably Cannes, to really get somewhere. You know, they now discuss film in the Iranian Parliament; that's how important it's become. It's a political issue to be a filmmaker.

JR: That's been especially true since the arrest of Tahmineh Milani a few days ago—because of her recent statements about the 1979 revolution to the press after the screening of her last film, *The Hidden Half*, which was shown at Fajr in February.

What kind of discussions do they have about films in Parliament?

MS: Well, sometimes they discuss the content and impact of films and sometimes you have controversy about particular films and different points of view, such as in which other countries a film is being seen and discussed. But earlier, in the first decade after the Revolution, when they weren't sure about a film policy, it was more of a political issue. Should we send this film outside or not? Of course now it's changed. Originally every film had to go through the Fajr Film Festival in order to get permission to be shown in foreign festivals—or even to be shown inside the country. Now certain films like Jafar Panahi's *The Circle* [2000] can get permission to get shown outside but not inside.

JR: You know, I'm hoping that, if this book gets translated into Farsi, it can answer certain questions in Iran as well as over here—such as what Americans see in Kiarostami. One American, anyway.

MS: Actually, while working with you, I'm realizing more that when you come from a different culture and history, you can appreciate certain things differently.

JR: Yes. I think an important part of your background, explaining where you're coming from—which you discuss briefly in your essay—is that you were the first Iranian to defend [Robert] Bresson in print, at least at any length. When was this?

MS: In 1978.

JR: So, right around the time of the Revolution.

MS: Yes, just a year before.

JR: I think, if I'm not mistaken, that he's a figure who is very important in Iran today—partially, I assume, because spiritual artists are valued highly, which is why one encounters so many references to [Fyodor] Dostoyevsky and [Franz] Kafka, for example. I also have this theory that Bresson's style rose in part out of his experience of having been a prisoner in an internment camp. I feel that his films are about souls in hiding—about keeping your humanity in a very private way in certain situations.

MS: It's a context in which people after the Revolution have come to appreciate his films. Sometimes you have to arrive at a condition to understand and appreciate certain things.

JR: I can realize now, looking at *Where Is the Friend's House?* [1986] again, that even though I was completely wrong to dismiss the film when I first saw it, one way in which I might have had a point is that it seems to be the last of the conventionally made features of Kiarostami's, at least from a narrative standpoint. What I mean is that the film has a narrative payoff—a moral, if you will—whereas the later films all leave out essential parts of the narrative. So maybe part of my response was reacting against the conventional aspect.

MS: Well, I think his other films all have payoffs. What about *Close-up*? I don't know how you can call it conventional or unconventional.

JR: *Close-up* begins unconventionally by starting off with the arrest of Sabzian and then not even showing that in a conventional manner.

MS: But there's still a payoff at the end. I know it doesn't have a conventional beginning and middle, but by the end of the film, there's a reconciliation between Makhmalbaf, the family, and the impersonator.

JR: I agree. When I was talking about payoff, I was thinking about films that were just fictional. You could say that *A.B.C. Africa* has a payoff at the end too.

MS: What I'm saying is that at the end of *Close-up*, it's a conventional payoff—it's not a symbolic or metaphorical or elliptical payoff or ending. And at the end of *Life and Nothing More . . .* [1992], the director character is a stranger who has been passing through all these villages without any real interaction, and then he decides to give a ride to this man who is carrying a very heavy canister.

JR: Can you really tell that's what's happening?

MS: Yes, in the long shot you can see it. Because the first time he passes by him and the second time he picks him up.

JR: Okay, I'll take your word for it. But the point I'm trying to make is that the first thing the film sets up is the expectation that he'll find out whether the kids he's looking for are alive or dead, but this never comes to pass. In other words, there's a displacement of payoff.

MS: Yes, it's true. But, you know, there's always a resolution at the end of his films, a payoff regarding his characters' struggles. In *Taste of Cherry*, for example, in order to create you have to go through hell. Yes, in order to bring birth to something you have to die first. You can call it anything you like, but it makes sense. Also, at the end of *Through the Olive Trees* [1994], it's only through that type of filmmaking and repetition and all that, that at the end the director notices Hossein is following Tahereh, he follows Hossein following the woman, and that becomes the natural ending for the film. The realization of this older man is his own attraction to the younger man, when he sees how far he goes after her. So in effect Hossein visualizes something for him to see. In the beginning he can't get it in his film. But he finally gets it offscreen, when the camera is no longer shooting.

JR: So you're saying that the last shot is a point-of-view shot?

MS: Yes, it is a point-of-view shot. Maybe not literally, but in effect, yes, it is. Just as one can talk about a kind of point of view shot at the end of *The Wind Will Carry Us.*

JR: But not in *Life and Nothing More . . .*

MS: No, there isn't one there. We look at him going up the hill in long shot. But when he throws the bone into the water at the end of *The Wind Will Carry Us,* it *is* some kind of shift.

JR: But you can't call it a point-of-view shot unless Behzad is running alongside the bone as it floats downstream.

MS: No. But what is not possible in real life becomes possible in film. The same thing applies to *Through the Olive Trees* and *Taste of Cherry,* too, where the hero has no control over his life and his environment, but then everything changes once it's seen as a film and he's seen as an actor. Also in *The Wind Will Carry Us,* where death doesn't happen in the film that he wants to shoot, but it happens just the same. And in *Through the Olive Trees,* what finally happens is what the director wanted to put in his film but couldn't.

JR: So, in other words, he sees something that stands for what he is missing in the film he is shooting. But I think we are in agreement if I say that the conventional payoff is displaced here, whereas the end in *Where Is the Friend's House?* is conventional.

MS: But when the boy is doing his homework near the end of the film, the audience doesn't know what he's actually doing. So what happens in the final scene isn't really a payoff.

JR: For me, the payoff is the irony of the teacher's remark: "Good boy." Because he thinks the boy has done his homework and we know that he hasn't. And the flower in a way takes the place of that homework and furnishes another payoff. It stands for a lot of things—for a gift that his friend has given to him, but also [for] the gift of the old man who makes doors. He gives it to the hero and says, "Put this in your notebook." So the payoff is a false recognition and a true recognition—in other words, a moral.

MS: But it's important that at the end of the film, there's no shot of the other boy, [Mohammad-Reza] Nematzadeh, appreciating it or reacting in any other way.

JR: I guess what I'm saying is that *Where Is the Friend's House?* becomes the last pedagogical film that Kiarostami made for Kanun, because each of the Kanun films is teaching you a lesson of some kind. And in this case what you're saying, and I agree, is that the lesson is not for the teacher but for us. But there's still a lesson there at the end.

MS: Yes, though it isn't the obvious one. As I mentioned to you earlier, in the original story that the film is based on, it's the teacher who notices what happens, and he breaks into tears. The story, in fact, is called "Why the Teacher Cried."[2] Probably he sees something he doesn't have. In this version, the only thing that's important is for the teacher not to punish the boy—and the other boy doesn't acknowledge that. Kiarostami shifts the emphasis onto the beloved rather than on the one who loves.

JR: I think what's interesting isn't that Kiarostami is eliminating the story in his later films. It's the reverse of that. He's basically showing that there is more story than you ever realized—

MS: —or that you expected.

JR: Yes, it's the story behind the story which is hidden and which he is trying to make evident. There are always more stories than you think there are, and the purpose of most conventional stories is to push these other stories out of the picture. Kiarostami is trying to bring them back.

MS: In all of his later films after *Where Is the Friend's House?* the scene before last becomes extremely important.

JR: Yes. In *The Wind Will Carry Us,* this is the scene in which Behzad takes the photos of those women.

MS: It's the scene before last that suggests a loss. In *Where Is the Friend's House?* it's the dark scene where he looks at the outside and at his mother in the wind. That could suggest fear of death, the unknown, night, or that his friend may be punished if he doesn't do anything. It opens up a whole set of mysteries and then shows you how trite it is to wrap up the story with one shot.

JR: Yes, it's so interesting. And there's a classical element in this scene, in the sense that the first time you see the boy with his mother is in the courtyard, when she's doing the wash. And she asks him to do all those things, too. What's interesting is, the only time in the whole film that she shows any kindness toward him is at night, just before the end of the film, when she's serving him dinner. For once, she isn't questioning him, either; she just assumes he's doing his own homework and not

Where Is the Friend's House?

his friend's. But the fact that the door suddenly blows open reminds us of that early scene and all the cruelty that she was showing toward him, and the other kinds of work he was asked to do.

MS: Yes, that scene opens a whole can of worms. (*Laughs.*) In fact, every time I see it, I have a different interpretation of it.

JR: It's formally quite brilliant, because the whole film clicks into place with that scene.

MS: Yes—without it, it would have been a very conventional film. But then that door opens to darkness.

JR: It's interesting to note that all the misunderstandings that grew out of the English subtitled version—calling the film *Where Is My Friend's House?* rather than *Where Is the Friend's House?*—isn't just a matter of overlooking the fact that it's named after a refrain in a poem [by Sohrab Sepehry]. It's also a matter of it being a philosophical question in the poem, not just a practical question. When I first saw the film, I missed the philosophical aspect. And the philosophical dimension is ultimately the same as the poetic dimension. Which is the most elusive part—and the part that he's after.

| | |

JR: Have you seen David Lynch's *The Straight Story* [1999]?

MS: Yes. Why?

JR: There's an American writer, Howard Hampton, who wrote an article in the January 2000 issue of *Artforum* called "Lynch Mob"—raising a ruckus because critics such as J. Hoberman, Kent Jones, and myself were too respectful of Hou Hsiao-hsien and Kiarostami and not respectful enough of *The Straight Story:*

> In its regard for ordinary people and the ways it finds to honor the mysteries of everyday life—along with the film's diffuse sense of time and its synthesis of almost pure visual abstraction and unadorned emotional intimacy—*The Straight Story* has obvious affinities with Iranian cinema's meld of realism and fable. But although the film was by and large enthusiastically if not perceptively received by mainstream reviewers, the serious critics who have championed like-minded foreign films were less generous, even condescending or outright dismissive. . . . Even a largely sympathetic reviewer like the *Chicago Reader*'s Jonathan Rosenbaum called the movie "propaganda," as if Lynch's taking money from Disney were inherently more compromising than Abbas Kiarostami's working under the aegis of a totalitarian theocracy.

There's plenty to object to here—such as associating Iranian cinema with "a diffuse sense of time" rather than the reverse of that.

MS: Maybe the reason why he thought that there was an affinity between *The Straight Story* and a group of Iranian films—in which I would *not* include Kiarostami's—is that there isn't a conventional dramatic structure. It's a simple plot. And there are some other similarities as well: the didactic moral values—which include family values—of this outdated hero, the dysfunctional women characters (all of whom help to point up his patriarchal wisdom), the backward ("third world") technology represented by the archaic vehicle that he drives, and the emphasis on landscape as a basis for spirituality.

JR: In other words, the eternal verities.

MS: But his linking of the supposed mysteries of everyday life in *The Straight Story* with those in Kiarostami seems false to me. What's so mysterious about the old man or the stereotypical people he encounters? He seems to be typecasting midwestern American farmers and Iranian peasants alike.

JR: His main argument should be examined more completely. He goes on to argue that

> *The Straight Story*'s headstrong old gentleman and the relentlessly single-minded protagonists of Kiarostami's films, or the equally determined

> little girl of Jafar Panahi's 1995, Kiarostami-scripted *White Balloon* (not to mention the upright, fiercely independent senior citizen Umberto D. of an earlier, no less allegorical branch of Neorealism), have an innate kinship—they are gnarled branches of the same cinematic family tree.
>
> Yet there is a widespread view among the film intelligentsia that humanity is the specialized province of the salt of the foreign earth, where indigenous cultures are typically mediated through familiar Eurocentric tropes and gestures (depoliticized avant-Godardisms, Bresson-oil rubdowns, the many moods of Antonioni). For these rigidly positioned film missionaries, places like Iowa are what they fly over on their pilgrimages to Lourdes-like film festivals—where true believers seek healing epiphanies, artistic "miracles," the blessings of directorial saints.

As offended as I was by Hampton's imputation of religious and Eurocentric motives to American defenses of Kiarostami and Hou Hsiao-hsien—as well as his facile swipe at Kiarostami's implied politics and his suggestion that some sort of "we are the world" humanism linking together *Umberto D.* [1952], *Taste of Cherry,* and *The Straight Story* is what actually makes all three films valuable—I have to concede now, as I wasn't willing to at the time, that he had a limited point in tracing a certain amount of anti-Americanism—or what I'd call a reaction against the arrogance of the American Empire—through our defenses of filmmakers like Kiarostami and Hou, neither of whom was incidentally receiving a hundredth as much attention as Lynch in the mainstream press.

MS: Do you think this is a cover-up for something else?

JR: Well, I wrote an angry letter to *Artforum* that was published [in the March 2000 issue] in which I accused Hampton of xenophobia, cold war thinking, and "indignant flag-waving"—basically "us" versus "them" thinking—and added, "What I'd like to know is where he sees propaganda for theocracy or totalitarianism in Kiarostami's work. And what does he mean, 'working under the aegis of,' especially when Lynch has to submit his work to test-marketing 'experts' and Kiarostami doesn't?"

Hampton replied [in the same issue of *Artforum*] that his "piece suggested that film critics no less than filmmakers need to be in some kind of empathetic touch with the everyday life and culture of their own land—if that's 'indignant flag-waving,' then I think Jean Renoir, Youssef Chahine, and the Ray boys (Nick and Satyajit) are equally 'xenophobic.'" I take it that what he meant by this—assuming that he was thinking and not indulging in more indignant flag-waving—was a kind of good or benign tribalism. My knee-jerk reaction to this—considering all that tribalism has meant and done over the past century and continues to do, and bearing in mind that I grew up in a small town in Alabama—is to regard such a notion as an oxymoron. (That's why I'm suspicious of a film like *Gabbeh* [1996]—in contrast to much better Makhmalbaf films like *Marriage of the Blessed* [1989] or more provocative ones like *Salaam Cinema* [1994], which I'd like to read as a polemical response to *Through the Olive Trees.*) But I'm probably being shortsighted about this. There must be cases of "good" tribalism that don't yield intolerance, even if I can't think of any.

MS: I think there's a very interesting distinction here. When I teach Iranian cinema and show in particular films by Kiarostami, students have a less defensive attitude; they're a little bit more open, and they relate to those topics better. Now I hate to make generalizations, but I think that some of the older generation have become more conservative. They have a certain contempt for the rest of the world, or for what they call the third world. I don't know how many times I've been regarded as a member of the third world, and automatically that's an insult, I assure you. It also has something to do with the economic and political relationship of one's own country to the country a film is coming from. For example, the relationship between Japan and the United States is very different from that between Iran and the United States.

JR: Well, as you know, when I recently wrote about *The Circle* for the *Chicago Reader,* I made a particular argument that my editor took out. I said the moment Coke machines are installed in Tehran, U.S. customs will stop fingerprinting and taking mug shots of every Iranian who comes here—a practice which, I should note, is not followed in Iranian customs when Americans enter that country, at least not when I went there in 2001. I call this cold war thinking too, because it's so paranoid.

MS: It's a very curious kind of threat when it comes to film. Because once you look at it from the other point of view, American film has monopolized the market in the rest of the world. So if those people in those countries are paranoid about Americans, there's at least some basis. (*Laughs.*)

JR: Yes—and sometimes the monopoly even turns out to be inadvertent. As you know, the most widely seen films in Iran are pirated dubs of brand new American movies on video that aren't even subtitled! Every film buff I spoke to seems to have her or his own dealer—a bit like the drug dealer who says, "I've got just the thing for you . . ."

In any case, if "good" tribalism *is* what Hampton had in mind by his list of "empathetic" filmmakers, his choice of examples couldn't be further off the mark. Renoir left France for Italy and then the United States during the war (and later made a film in India, *The River* [1951]), eventually settling permanently in Los Angeles—and some French critics never forgave him for this act of desertion. Chahine emigrated to the United States as a teenager himself, and his films are full of American (and French) references. Nick Ray made films about Romany and Inuit people (*Hot Blood* [1956] and *The Savage Innocents* [1960]) and ended his commercial filmmaking career in Europe. And even Satyajit Ray had the brash idea of making at least one picture, *The Chess Players* [1997], in Hindi and English rather than in Bengali. Similarly, Kiarostami has now also broken Hampton's golden rule by making a documentary in Uganda that's principally in English, rather than sticking to his own tribe and remaining "in some kind of empathetic touch with the everyday life and culture of his own land"—a land Hampton has already defined as "a totalitarian theocracy."

My point is that Americans have no right to view Kiarostami principally as an Iranian artist if we don't know what being Iranian—as opposed to, say, Islamic (assuming that we know that either)—really consists of. And is Hampton really sure he knows all the ramifications of what Lynch being an American means, especially for people outside the United States? Or is he interested in Americans speaking only for themselves and to themselves, as they are sometimes wont to do?

MS: But is Hampton very far away from Roger Ebert? It's an important part of American culture to be so Eurocentric, and that's reflected in American film criticism. There's also the bigger issue of the art film in general. Think how seriously some Americans take *Memento* [2001]—a completely empty, superficial film as opposed to *The Circle,* which was running at the same time. It's just part of a general problem that people have trouble with films that aren't sentimental or obvious. Look at the films that are so popular here, even among the Iranian ones.

JR: Isn't part of that a resistance to political films?

MS: Yes, and not only ones from Iran. I don't know who said it, but it's been argued that the people who appreciate art the best are the censors. They know what's good—and they censor it! (*Laughs.*)

JR: What about Hampton's charge that I was automatically placing Kiarostami on some loftier plain because I was describing *The Straight Story* as "propaganda," but not *Taste of Cherry*?

MS: Even some Iranians share that point of view. Do you know how many people have attacked me for helping the Chicago Film Center bring films from Iran? Those Iranians who think that they're dissidents say that *any* film from Iran is propaganda. I say, if you think like that, you shouldn't show any film from any country in the world, including the United States. You have to look at a particular film to see what it has to say in order to decide whether it's propaganda or not.

JR: Yes. You could also say by the same logic that the few American films that have been allowed commercial runs in Iran in recent years—such as *Seven* [1995], *Dances with Wolves* [1990], and *The Godfather* [1972]—must also be propaganda on behalf of the Islamic government (*Laughs.*) I mean, why those films? It all looks pretty suspicious.

MS: I think there *is* a problem outside the United States. Because of the way it's monopolized the market in cinema, weapons, and other products, some people do have this anti-American bias. But that doesn't stop the ordinary audience from appreciating a good American film—they'll go and see it and won't take it as propaganda. And if certain people in the government call it propaganda, that's a very narrow-minded type of judgment that I think is very dangerous. It becomes a mask for hatred and fear. You know, when *Taste of Cherry* received the main prize in Cannes, the way Roger Ebert talked about the film made it seem like it was just a political prize. He was very disappointed.

JR: Yes, he was so disaffected that he hasn't seen any other Kiarostami film since then—or at least he hasn't reviewed any. He basically wrote that he thought the film was a fraud: "I thought I had seen an emperor without any clothes."[3]

MS: And he isn't the only one: there are Iranians who think that. So it's not a question of the film's nationality. It's the character of the film that does something to you. First of all, I think it's a question of class. Then it's a question of life experience and maturity. Most of the films that Roger Ebert likes are pretty sentimental. They're paternalistic. I'm not crazy about the films critics like him tend to like from India, Iran, or wherever. They're most often tearjerkers about pitiful little boys and poor helpless women.

JR: Let me play devil's advocate. You've argued very persuasively in your essay that many of Kiarostami's films are about the exploitation and abuse of children. Couldn't Roger reply to you that this is what some of Majid Majidi's films are also about?

MS: I think Majidi's films are more accessible; you can cry while watching them. But in a film like *The Traveler* [1974], the way Kiarostami shows you the child, he doesn't encourage you to cry. It's much deeper than that.

JR: Would you call his films intellectual? Because some of what we're encountering against Kiarostami is anti-intellectualism.

MS: There are very strong intellectual layers in his films, but I cannot call him an intellectual—not in the way that term is generally understood.

JR: That's a good distinction. But some people who don't like his films very much tend to regard them as intellectual just the same. The same thing happened to Jacques Tati—who was even less of an intellectual than Kiarostami is. At least Kiarostami is capable of quoting [the Romanian writer] E. M. Cioran, for instance.

But I better watch out and not turn Eurocentric, though Hampton is far from being the only American critic who insists on reading Eastern or Middle Eastern filmmakers through European filters (which include Christianity and Catholicism, both prominent reference points in his attack). In fact, my original review of *Taste of Cherry* [June 14, 1996] in the *Chicago Reader* was designed to get beyond such stereotypes; I began by comparing Kiarostami to Tati, Bresson, Godard, and Michelangelo Antonioni only to conclude later that these references might be essential to me—as routes into his work, and maybe even as security blankets—but that didn't mean they were essential to him. Unfortunately, in one article Godfrey Cheshire quoted the first part of my argument without ever bringing up the second part.[4]

MS: What do they mean when they call someone an intellectual? It depends on what's hidden behind the term. Sometimes they want to call Kiarostami an intellectual so they can dismiss him.

JR: That's a peculiarly American notion—that you're out of touch with ordinary experience if you think. And what's so weird in this country is that it's unconsciously connected to a class position.

MS: Those things aren't just American. They're Iranian too.

JR: I guess I'm being American in the worst sense—that is, automatically assuming that some local traits are unique. But I see what you mean: shortsightedness is actually universal. This reminds me of the question that so many people in Tehran asked me: is it true that Americans like Iranian art movies because they show so many poor people, which is the way most Americans want to see Iran? My usual response was, "Maybe there are too many poor people in Iranian art films. But there are also too many rich people in the American commercial movies you watch on video, and if you think you're getting an accurate picture of American life that way, you're just as mistaken as we are."

MS: But Americans don't really care, because they're in the position of power, so it doesn't matter if their self-image is mutilated. But the rest of the world can't afford that—do you know what I'm saying? In the same way, the head of a company can wear sandals and a T-shirt to work, but not his employees.

Now, to bring Kiarostami to the same level as some American independent filmmakers—although they are not all that independent—such as David Lynch is an insult, it's a cultural attack. How dare you bring in somebody like that! It's interesting that in Europe you won't find such megalomania. They can accept you, fine. But here—

JR: Yes. Though to be precise, Hampton isn't dismissing Kiarostami because he's an intellectual, as we might have implied earlier. I think what he's suggesting is that, on the contrary, he can be acceptable—*if* he becomes American. Not European, the way he thinks critics like Hoberman, Jones, and I regard him, and certainly not Iranian, but American. All he has to do is 'fess up and agree that he's the blood brother of David Lynch.

Maybe Hampton thinks I'm being snobbish because I don't consider *Taste of Cherry* and *The Straight Story* "like-minded films." For me, imposing such a connection eliminates almost everything I like in both films while making them seem sappier than they actually are.

MS: I want to speak about something that's very difficult for Iranians in this country. Look at the situation of Kiarostami: some people in

Iran tell him he just makes films for foreigners. And some foreigners say he should be appreciated mainly in his own country. They push him from both sides, making him homeless. Or look at the case of [Sohrab Shahid] Saless. He left Iran during the shah's time. He lived in Germany twenty-five years and made fourteen films there. But when he died, all the German publications called him an Iranian filmmaker.

Okay. Then, when I spoke to Simon Field three years ago about showing a retrospective of his films at the Rotterdam Film Festival, he said, "But he's not Iranian—he made most of his films in Germany." So he can't be appreciated as part of any national cinema. What does that say about "us"?

I need to make a distinction. A lot of immigrants to this country came from Europe. There's a very strong affinity with European culture, and in fact it's very Eurocentric here. It's not much of a difficulty for a European to come here and establish himself or herself as an artist. But a person from the Middle East? God forbid! An Iranian who wants to come here?

JR: It's obviously much harder. But even for Europeans, there's an enormous pressure to give up one's background.

MS: For Middle Easterners in the West, their clichéd image always precedes them. Do you know that I just received an offer to direct a commercial for Dutch TV? They said they wanted it in "Iranian film style"! And look at what people are called: "African-Americans," "Mexican-Americans." Yet those who come from Europe—meaning white people—aren't hyphenated. If Kiarostami were European, Hampton would probably have a different attitude toward him.

Why does a critic who considers himself an intellectual feel he has to defend only his national culture? I think it's a very dangerous position.

In my classes, I've sometimes said, "Okay, close your eyes. When I say 'Iran,' what's the first thing that comes into your head? Is it a language you don't understand? Looks? Clothes? Landscape? And if we rule these things out, what's left? Big cities in the so-called third world are polluted, just as they're polluted here. Nature and human emotions are the same. Human ambitions are universal. It all boils down to attitudes and politics that condition us to see others as being separate from ourselves."

During Operation Desert Storm, when these little maps of the Middle East were everywhere—even around public swimming pools, with arrows indicating where we were fighting—my students would ask me, "How is your family now?" I'd say, "I'm not from Iraq," and they'd say, "Sorry"—even though 99 percent of them thought that Iraq should be bombed back to the Stone Age. But this country, apart from its own civil war, has never been through the social disaster of a war on its own soil and what this means on a daily basis. That's why war for them remains an abstraction. You know, when students can't pronounce my name, I remind them that they can learn and pronounce Arnold Schwarzenegger's name—so they should be able to learn mine.

Addenda: Reflections on 10, June 9, 2002, Chicago

JR: A lot has happened since we provisionally completed this book with the preceding dialogue: first, the [September 11] terrorist attacks on the World Trade Center and the Pentagon, and, following this event, many contradictory responses—some suggesting that the United States is now closer to the remainder of the world than it was before (in terms of danger and suffering), and some, on the contrary, appearing to intensify American isolationism, as typified by George W. Bush's "axis of evil" speech early this year. One of the immediate consequences of the latter is [that it is] even harder for certain suspicious "axis of evil" types like Kiarostami—that is, all Iranian citizens—to visit the United States than it was before.

MS: The Senate recently passed a bill to refuse even study or tourist visas to citizens of Middle Eastern countries—not counting Israel, of course.

JR: On the other hand, there appears to be a greater curiosity in the West about the Middle East, as evidenced by enormous turnouts late last year in Chicago for various public events relating to Afghanistan.

Kiarostami's latest feature, *10* [2002]—which premiered at Cannes last month, and which we've just been able to see on video—indirectly seems to address this new situation by telling us more about life in contemporary Tehran than any of his previous features, at least since *Report* [1977], almost as if it were a precious message placed in a bottle and sent out into the world. And the bottle in this case is a DV [digital video] camera—or, more precisely, what appear to have been two DV cameras mounted on the dashboard of a car, usually affording separate camera angles of the driver (a young, recently divorced and remarried woman) and her various passengers, in ten sequences numbered in descending order: her ten-year-old son Amin (in sequences 10, 5, 3, and 1); a woman friend she's going to a restaurant with (4); her sister (9); and three strangers she gives lifts to—an old woman who's going to a shrine (8), a prostitute (7), and a young woman she gives two separate lifts to away from the same shrine (6 and 2). As you've pointed out, these ten sequences, which take place over an indeterminate stretch of time, could almost be appearing in reverse chronological order—though not quite, because it's made clear in the dialogue that 2 occurs after 6, when the driver meets the young woman for the first time. The sequences all begin with a number and the sound of a bell, like at a sports event, which has a distancing and formalizing effect. Kiarostami has indicated that part of his aim in this film—a daring enterprise—is to see if direction can be eliminated from fiction filmmaking.

MS: It's not eliminated, but it's reduced to a minimum, because Kiarostami isn't visible inside the car to control the improvised dialogue and performances.

JR: It's roughly analogous to the scene in *Touch of Evil* [1958] with Charlton Heston and Mort Mills driving through town in an open convertible. Welles didn't come along for the ride because he wanted to be surprised by what the actors did.

MS: It's also a highly provocative application of Kiarostami's idea that in cinema, amateurs sometimes have better ideas than professionals, and it extends not only the immediacy of the DV camera but also the democratic possibilities—it's significant that he makes no separation between the actors and the crew in the final credits. It also has some of the intimacy of home video and some of the surreptitiousness of the surveillance camera. It's interesting that for Kiarostami, the car often functions as the ultimate private space—a very modern idea—yet the use of the surveillance camera in public space interferes with this. Ever since September 11, surveillance cameras are everywhere, like wiretaps; all private space is up for grabs.

When passengers, especially Amin, accidentally look at the camera while they're speaking, it creates some uncomfortable moments, because it seems like they're addressing the audience. It also changes the way some audiences value what they're seeing in terms of art; some people have had a relatively low opinion of the last sequences of *Taste of Cherry*, of *A.B.C. Africa*, and now of this film because of the video, which they associate with journalism.

JR: If anyone proves that journalism can be an art, it's Kiarostami. Look at *Homework* [1988] and *Close-up*. It's still too soon to know what I really think of *10*, but I think it's already clear that it's journalism in a good sense.

MS: Deborah Young wrote in her review of the film in *Variety* [May 27–June 2, 2002] that he spent several weeks before the shoot rehearsing with the nonprofessional actors, and he himself, in the statement he gave out in Cannes [see the interviews in this volume], compares his role to that of a football coach—which may help to account for the bell between each sequence.

JR: By limiting his choices to two camera angles, he shows how many expressive possibilities are still there in the filmmaking and editing choices. The virtual absence of reverse angles in 10, 8, and 7—so that we don't see the driver until after her son leaves [the car], we don't see the prostitute until after she leaves the car, and we barely see the old woman [at all]—gives all three of these characters a special kind of weight in these segments that they wouldn't have if they were visible. And the characters we do see appear to be harassed by the camera—such as Amin in the first sequence, who reminds me of the boy who cries at the end of *Homework*.

MS: I only wish there had been at least one middle-aged woman; restricting the cast to young women and one very old woman—who seems there to impart wisdom the way that old men function in other Kiarostami films—implicitly becomes a statement about Iran's younger generation. The fact that the leading character is a woman who's left her own marriage seems quite significant.

JR: And yet her son makes this an excuse to blame her for everything.

MS: The anger of the son toward the mother reflects not only his father's attitude but the attitude of an entire culture toward any woman who takes the initiative in a divorce, in pursuit of her own interests. It's pathetic and disturbing that a mother should need the approval of her own son in this matter, as if he were the father.

JR: Why do we see two of her passengers, as well as her, going to a shrine—which is confusingly called a mausoleum in the subtitles of the version we saw?

MS: The word is *emamzadeh,* which means a saint's shrine. On the surface, it's a cultural routine, but not for the younger generation—unless they're inspired by the older generation, as you see here. The fact that the driver isn't wearing makeup both times she's giving a lift to the younger woman shows that she's just been to the shrine as well—which is one of the many signs in the film that she's unhappy, quite possibly with her second marriage as well as with the partial loss of her child.

JR: What is it about her bond with this younger woman? There almost seems to be something flirtatious between the women when she shows the driver her shaved head in the second scene.

MS: The film also plays on the idea of lesbians in the scene with the prostitute. But that wasn't my reaction to this scene. I saw the driver admiring her because of the strength, integrity, and self-containment of her silent suffering and secret rebellion, which is basically selfless. She reminded me of [Carl] Dreyer's Falconetti and also of the woman who unveils her shaved head in Makhmalbaf's *Marriage of the Blessed.* Apart from the driver, she's the only one in the film who's mysterious.

JR: It's quite a contrast with her friend—who's also just ended a relationship, who cries incessantly, and whom the driver can't tolerate or give any comfort to at all. This kind of intimacy that can be established only with strangers reminds me of *Taste of Cherry.*

MS: But the central character in that film had a goal.

JR: She's identified as a photographer and a painter who travels a lot as well as something of a religious skeptic, which clearly places her in the designated "Kiarostami" role—the middle-class driver and questioner engaging with people from different walks of society; it's interesting that Kiarostami originally thought of making her a psychoanalyst, driving with her patients (see the interviews in this volume). The only question is whether we believe in her as a real person—a question also raised for me by her friend who's crying.

MS: The driver certainly breaks the usual Western stereotype of the Iranian woman as religious and servile; she's a rebellious woman, even if she's also victimized, so that the complexity of Iranian society is really exposed here, regardless of whether she's real or not. In spite of all the talk about national differences since September 11, most of the issues here are universal. And Kiarostami's use of ellipsis has become even more relevant by creating a context for discussion and audience interaction, which is now needed more than ever.

JR: I find *10* less emotionally affecting than Kiarostami's other recent features, yet fascinating as an experiment. And the emotional responses it evokes are part of what's being experimented with. Do you remember Kiarostami telling us, the first time we interviewed him together [in March 1998], that men who saw *Through the Olive Trees* tended to think that the woman in the last shot said yes to Hossein, while most women thought she didn't? I was reminded of that when we discussed our separate responses to the first sequence in *10:* you were highly irritated by the way the mother speaks to Amin, but I was just as irritated by the way Amin speaks to her; I find him obnoxious and bossy—a male chauvinist in miniature. Does this subjectivity have anything to do with the fact that you're a parent and I'm not? I have no idea. But the fact that we both had strong reactions seems even more important.

MS: I'm irritated with Amin in other scenes. But the offscreen voice of the mother bombarding her child with her own issues in the opening sequence, the longest in the film, prevented me from having sympathy for this beautiful woman—whom we don't realize is beautiful until we see her at the end of the sequence. And her beauty functions in a way as her mask. Like all of Kiarostami's main characters, she's basically inaccessible.

Notes

1. Postscript, August 2002: One example of this, which may in this case have started outside Iran, is rumors regarding a short film Kiarostami was originally contracted to make for a feature of ten-minute sketches by different directors entitled *Ten Minutes Older,* which premiered at the Cannes Film Festival in May 2002. The coauthors decided to omit this item from this book's filmography after having been told that Kiarostami never delivered his short film. A subsequent unverified rumor, heard just as this book was going to press, maintained that Kiarostami in fact did make a short film consisting of a single shot of a little boy sleeping, but the film's producers decided not to include it in the feature.

2. Behruz Tajuar's "Cherz Khanum Moallem Geryeh Kard."

3. Roger Ebert, *Roger Ebert's Movie Yearbook 2000* (Kansas City: Andrews McNeel Publishing, 2000), 594.

4. Godfrey Cheshire, "How to Read Kiarostami," *Cineaste* 25.4 (2000): 9–10.

Interviews with Abbas Kiarostami

Unless otherwise noted, all of Kiarostami's statements in this chapter are translated from Persian.

March 1998, Chicago

JONATHAN ROSENBAUM: It seems that your films were appreciated in France before they were appreciated in most other places. Why do you think this happened?

ABBAS KIAROSTAMI: Only because [the French] were more attentive. They put aside their differences and looked at the films with open minds. They didn't change the substance of the films in any way, but they pay more attention. When I say audiences are similar, that doesn't mean that they look at films with the same attentiveness. In my own country, Iran, they pay less attention because they haven't yet outgrown the tradition of melodrama, and they're still in awe of Hollywood because they haven't yet experienced it fully. In my country, people go to films for only two reasons: to laugh or to cry. And naturally, I can't compare this audience to the French audience.

JR: In this respect, the American audience is similar to the Iranian audience.

MEHRNAZ SAEED-VAFA: People go either to laugh or cry everywhere.

AK: I know, but I was discussing a particular section of the audience who looks for a different kind of film in Iran, the United States, and Europe.

JR: I feel that a problem all over the world is how to reach this section, because the media are preoccupied almost exclusively with commercial films. There's also an enormous amount of misinformation about Iranian cinema.

MS: (*to JR*) What do you think the role of the critic is regarding this? Do you feel that, compared with the major distributors and producers, they don't have much power?

JR: Sometimes they can. For me, the most important role of the critic is conveying information. Last year, when I faxed you [AK] that letter about my worry that you were going to cut the ending of *Taste of Cherry* [1997] before it opened here—which you were kind enough to reply to right away—this [rumor] was something I'd heard from several professional critics, some of whom even approved of the idea. And since then, I've heard the same false story repeated many times. There are a lot of these false impressions floating around.

MS: When Godfrey Cheshire wrote an article for the *New York Times* last fall [September 28, 1997] to promote the film, he said that because Islamic law prohibits suicide, Kiarostami had a lot of trouble with the Islamic government.

JR: Roger Ebert just implied the same thing in the *Chicago Sun-Times* two days ago.

AK: Actually, I like to have this kind of interpretation in conversations and dialogue around my films.

JR: Well, some of it can be good, but some of it can be damaging. The problem is, there's a constant confusion between criticism and advertising, and sometimes your films become the victims of false advertising.

AK: When this interpretation is in the hands of the mass media, who can control it anyway? And sometimes critics and journalists want to misunderstand.

JR: Maybe this happens more often with your films because of the missing pieces in your narratives. Instead of audiences filling these empty spaces, the publicists and journalists fill them.

AK: In any case, it's better to be deceived by these others than by the filmmakers. There's always a chance that audiences will think about those parts and find their own solutions.

JR: Do many false rumors about your films circulate in Iran?

AK: It happens to most films, not only mine. People are living with those rumors. For example, if they announce that I'll be appearing after the film and then for some reason I get stuck in traffic, they'll automatically think I've been arrested. Because they need to have these stories. It's not only in cinema: rumors are a major source for finding out about other people's problems. Most of these rumors are about secret sexual liaisons, and these show how much people need to affirm that these relationships exist, despite the prohibitions. When I heard the recent stories about [Bill] Clinton, this showed me that it could happen anywhere, that people need to think that he's a human being who can make mistakes like anyone else.

JR: Yes, this [the Bill Clinton and Monica Lewinsky story] is the most popular American "movie" right now.

MS: Did you arrive at your principles of ellipsis and omission gradually, through your experience of making films?

AK: Yes. When I was screening *Homework* [1988], a member of the audience who was a well-known figure came up to me and thanked me and then suggested that maybe I could make my films better by depending less on my personal experience and thinking more about film as a way of documenting, where the audience can use it as a kind of reference. That's when I first thought about writing a different kind of documentary, where the audience could put the pieces together on their own. When you go to a supermarket, everybody has a different purchasing power, so everyone shouldn't come away with the same product. In the same way, when you see a film, you should come away with your own personal interpretation, based on who you are. The film should allow that to happen, make room for that interaction.

JR: I associate that kind of interaction with the fact that you shoot a great deal of your action in long shot. In most commercial films, close-ups tend to fill up the open spaces you're describing. It may have a little to do with what [Charlie] Chaplin meant when he said that comedy is long shot and tragedy is close-up.

AK: When the woman stops walking in the last sequence of *Through the Olive Trees* [1994], audiences invent their own close-ups without me providing any because of their own attentiveness to what's happening. They furnish the meaning of the event.

JR: Your method of shooting corresponds to this. The fact that none of the major actors in *Taste of Cherry* met one another during the shooting meant that each of them was imagining a different character he was speaking or listening to. So it's a principle used in the making of your films, not just in the viewing of them.

AK: You have to follow that because your actors are precious; they're your first audience, so they have to be participating in the same process.

MS: Did you inform the actors in *Taste of Cherry* when you were shooting and when you were just rehearsing?

AK: No, there was no film crew there. They would set up the camera for me in the car, because I was the only one around apart from the actor [i.e., I was serving as the stand-in for the character the actor was speaking or listening to].

JR: Did the actors have to memorize their lines?

AK: Nothing was written—it was all spontaneous. I would control certain parts and get them to say certain lines, but it was basically improvisation.

JR: So were all these actors speaking as themselves?

AK: Not exactly. The actor playing the soldier wasn't a soldier; I prompted him beforehand about the location of the army camp, for example. The film was a combination of real and unreal. For instance, I ordered some guns, so the actor thought he'd get a chance to shoot one of them later on, when we were filming, and he didn't realize that this kind of instruction was the actual filming. He was even getting anxious and asking when the filming would start. I actually made him believe I was planning to kill myself.

It reminds me of a verse from the poet Rumi:

> You are my polo ball,
> running before the stick of my command

I am always running along after you,
though it is I who make you move.

JR: Is this similar to the technique you used in *Homework*?

AK: Yes, though that was in a more documentary context. The most important part of the technique is to connect all the reactions—to knot them all together. Sometimes there's no way to relate them to one another.

JR: It seems to have something in common with jazz. Maybe that's why I like your use of Louis Armstrong playing "St. James Infirmary" in the final sequence of *Taste of Cherry*.

AK: Exactly. Because even though you're following certain notes, you're also following the feeling of the piece, so the performance you're giving tonight will be different from the performance tomorrow.

JR: It's also about playing together.

AK: Yes, but these actors can't have a dialogue with each other because one part is always played by me.

JR: Right—you're the composer and the bandleader.

AK: At one point, I wanted the soldier character to express amazement, but since I couldn't ask him to do that, I started to speak to him in Czech. He said he couldn't understand what I was talking about, and I used that in the film. At another point, I placed a gun in the glove compartment and asked him to open it for a chocolate, when I wanted him to look afraid.

JR: Have you worked with professional actors on some of your other films?

AK: Only on one film—with the man who played the film director in *Through the Olive Trees*.

JR: One thing that *Taste of Cherry* conveys very powerfully is the experience of being alone, and your method of shooting intensifies that sense of isolation.

AK: There are signs in the film that sometimes made me think that the man didn't really want to kill himself, that he was looking for a kind of communication with the other characters. Maybe that's one of the ruses of his loneliness, to engage people with his own emotional issues. He doesn't pick up a couple of workers at the beginning who would be willing to kill him with their spades; he chooses other people whom he probably thinks he can have a conversation with. So that gives us a signal that he's probably not searching for someone who would help him to kill himself.

JR: It's also interesting how your images metaphorically reproduce the situation of the spectator watching the film. In many of your films, the view through a car's windshield represents that situation—of looking for something but also feeling separate from what you're looking at.

AK: That comes from my experience of driving around Tehran in my car and sometimes driving outside the city—looking through the front, rear, and side windows, which become my frames.

May 2000, San Francisco

JR: When did you first use your technique of working alone with your actors, without scripted dialogue?

AK: It's a good thing that I saw *The Traveler* [1974] again last night [at the San Francisco Film Festival], because that's where it all started.

JR: Did you have a partial script for that film?

AK: We did have a script, with the lines divvied up between the actors. The parts of the old woman and the school principal were written in a particular Iranian dialect; I gave the actors precise lines and asked them to memorize them. The old woman couldn't read or write, but with the aid of her grandchild she could memorize the lines. But by the time we started shooting, she'd learned her lines so well that she also knew the principal's lines. Then when we tried to make her forget the principal's lines and say just her own, she had problems, because she'd memorized the dialogue like a computer, without any thought of what it meant. So we finally had to let her go and we found someone else to play the old woman—someone who couldn't memorize lines but could comprehend them and understand the character's part. And at the time we were dependent on dubbing, but in order to work with the woman more spontaneously, we had to shoot with direct sound. This was one of the first times this was done in Iran, apart from [Ebrahim] Golestan's *Brick and Mirror* [1965], which tried unsuccessfully to use the same technique. He could afford the sound equipment that was needed, but most Iranian filmmakers couldn't.

JR: There's an interesting parallel to this with Taiwanese cinema in *City of Sadness* [1989]. I've heard that Hou Hsiao-hsien introduced direct sound to Taiwanese cinema in order to record the voice of his friend Li Tien-lu, whose life later became the subject of *The Puppetmaster* [1993]—specifically Li's idiosyncratic delivery and his regional dialect. So, if I understand this correctly, the motivation is somewhat similar: the desire to let people speak more naturally in their own voices.

AK: What was crucial was that from then onward, whenever I had nonprofessional actors, I got them to extemporize, the same way that we're talking now, rather than memorize lines. The problem with this was that the noise created by the film equipment, which didn't have the capabilities needed for precise synchronization, made it difficult to get a precise match between sound and image in the editing. So we had to wrap a kind of comforter around the camera to mute the sounds made by the vibrations.

JR: I'm curious about a particular moment in *The Wind Will Carry Us* [1999], when the hero asks the little boy, "Do you think I'm a bad man?" and the little boy blushes and says, "No, I don't think you're a bad man." When I saw that, I had the impression that it was you asking the boy precisely that question. Is that correct?

AK: Yes, I was behind the camera and I asked him that question.

JR: It does seem very much like a personal response from the boy that isn't an actor's response, and for me it was a very important moment.

AK: I had to ask him that question because he didn't like me very much in contrast to the actor who was playing the main character. So that's why he wasn't very convincing when he called me a good man! (*Laughter.*)

JR: Yes, he was blushing and very fidgety. So were there only some scenes with the boy where you used this technique or did you always use it?

AK: I always used it, except for when you see two people speaking in the same shot or when the person is on the telephone. When he's on the phone, the method is always that I speak first and the character repeats what I say. And the time he has to wait for the answers to his questions allows him to listen to what I'm saying and just repeat it.

JR: Were you yourself carrying a mobile phone while you were shooting the film?

AK: It wouldn't have even worked there—it was too remote. In order for a real mobile to have worked, you would have had to climb the equivalent of two mountains.

MS: I know that locations are very important for you, and I heard that you spent two months looking for the village in *The Wind Will Carry Us*.

AK: Longer. Two years is more like it.

MS: What sort of village were you looking for?

AK: It wasn't simply a matter of it being in Kurdistan. I also wanted there to be an element of surprise. In a way I was searching just like the characters in the movie when they're looking for the location.

JR: How did you get the idea for that scene when the apple rolls down from one level of the village to another?

AK: In my book of poems [*Walking with the Wind*], which was recently published [in Iran]—although I'm still waiting for the corrected edition to come out—there's a poem about the experience that brought me to the scene with the apple. It happened a long time before this film. I saw a fruit seller with a stand that included apples, and when I started to pick one up, it fell off and rolled down the street to a spot where two young men were seated. And as soon as it rolled by, without looking to see where it came from or whom it belonged to, one of the young men picked it up, cleaned it off with his shirt, and bit into it.

MS: It's a familiar moment in your films. I'm thinking of the moment in *Close-up* [1990] when the guy kicks the spray can across the pavement.

AK: There's also something like that in the first scene of my first film, *Bread and Alley* [1970], and in *Solution* [1978], when someone's rolling a tire down a highway.

JR: What the scene with the apple in *The Wind Will Carry Us* suggests to me is that the village has a hidden structure that outsiders don't know. This makes me want to ask you, If you spent two years looking for this village, what were you looking for?

AK: I was looking for a village with a strange architectural design—something that would seem strange to the viewer as well as to us, suggesting a strangeness that would be brought out by the local funeral ceremony. When I found this village, it was so remote that when we went back to the place to begin shooting, we had some trouble finding it.

JR: It's similar in a way to the village the boy travels to in *Where Is the Friend's House?* [1986], where the buildings seem to cling precariously to the side of the hill.

AK: This is a common trait, and it comes from the days when villagers built their houses that way to protect themselves from the elements, so that the rain, for example, would slide off.

MS: You spoke earlier to me [in Tehran] about the kinds of experiences you had that led to writing poetry. Could you speak some more about those experiences?

AK: The poetry came to me while I was filming. I did get some inspiration from the dialogue, but the reverse was also true—sometimes the poetry inspired the dialogue.

Regarding the poem by Forugh [Farrokhzad] that I used in the film, when I read it this time, it made much more sense to me than it had before. I could see that its philosophy and themes were close to Omar Khayyám's philosophy of life and death.

JR: In what way?

AK: Both have a view of death in which life is only temporary, so that you should enjoy life while you can. Forugh was only thirty-two when she died, and she wrote this poem when she was thirty. She did have a view of how transitory life is.

JR: One thing that seems very important about the scene in which this poem is quoted to a woman milking a cow is that it's the only one in the film set inside a real interior; everything else is outdoors. I also think it's important that in your last few films, almost no scenes take place inside—unless you count the scenes inside cars.

AK: I wanted to show the pit of an interior—not just a roof over someone's head but a place that was dark and underground.

JR: It's very powerful, because it rhymes with the hole this woman's fiancé is inside while he's digging on the hill.

AK: Yes, that was the idea. Death is the constant theme of the movie. That's why I placed that scene in the darkness and deep inside the earth, not merely inside a house.

JR: One interesting idea I find in your last several films is that being inside signifies privacy and being outside means being in public. Being in a car with open windows is a way of being both inside and outside, in the same way that movie theaters are both public places and private places. Because everyone sees a film with an audience *and* as an individual, with private responses, one can say that there's the same ambiguity about what's public and what's private in a movie theater.

AK: I'll have to think about that. It's a critic's idea. I might have been thinking something like this unconsciously, but it's hard to say.

JR: There's a parable by Plato that sees the shadows on the wall of a cave as a representation of reality. It can be read as a kind of metaphor about cinema, and this scene reminds me very much of that metaphor.

AK: My intention in this film and in my previous films is to show signs of reality that viewers won't necessarily comprehend but will nonetheless feel. Basically anything seen through a camera limits the view of a spectator to what's visible through the lens, which is always much less than we can see with our own eyes. No matter how wide we make the screen, it still doesn't compare to what our eyes can see of life. And the only way out of this dilemma is sound. If you show the viewer it's like peeking through a keyhole, that it's just a limited view of a scene, then the viewer can imagine it, imagine what's beyond the reach of his eyes. And viewers do have creative minds. If, for example, we don't see anything but hear the sound of a car suddenly screeching to a halt and then hitting something, we automatically have a picture of the accident in our mind's eye. The viewer always has this curiosity to imagine what's outside the field of vision; it's used all the time in everyday life. But when people come to a theater they've been trained to stop being curious and imaginative and simply take what's given to them. That's what I'm trying to change.

JR: I wonder if this is a key to what's different in your sound conception for *The Wind Will Carry Us.* It seems like the field of what we hear is much larger than the field of what we see and that the discrepancy between the two is much larger than in your previous films. Is that true? Is the canvas of what one hears much larger?

AK: The sound is supposed to assume the role of what isn't visible. Throughout this movie it was a challenge to see if we could show without showing, to show what's invisible, and to show it in the minds of the viewers rather than on the screen. And there was a desire also to go against what everyday entertainment movies do—the trend of showing an audience everything to the point of being pornographic. I don't mean sexually pornographic, but pornographic in the sense of showing open-heart surgery in all its gory details. I feel that whenever the viewer has the impulse to turn his head or avert his eyes, these are the unnecessary scenes that have been presented. My way of framing the action actually makes the viewers sit up straighter and try to stretch their necks so they can try to see whatever I'm not showing! There are similar scenes in Hou Hsiao-hsien's movies when he shows a character disappearing from the frame but is still talking, and you know that the character is still there, even if he's only sensed, felt, or heard. Just like someone can be next door in the bathroom; you don't see them, but you know they're there. It's that feeling that the viewer would sense the presence of a character rather than see him that I wanted to create.

JR: It's like the idea of [Robert] Bresson's that whenever you can, you replace an image with a sound.

AK: In fact, I've studied all his films for precisely that reason.

It's true that the world is shrinking and things are becoming more and more similar because so much is being exchanged. Everything's being globalized: for example, when I was recently in Africa, I was looking to buy a few souvenirs to take back with me, and I saw mostly the same things I saw in Paris and other places. Things seem to be losing those specific characteristics they used to have that separate one area or nation from another. The only exception to that rule, luckily, is human nature. Certain rules govern the growth of trees; they need light, water, dirt, and air. By the same token, there are things that all people need. It's our good fortune that all the superficial things have become so superficial that only human nature provides us with a refuge that has any depth to it.

MS: I wasn't quite clear about the relation you described earlier between your poetry and your filmmaking. You seemed to be saying that some of your poems influenced your dialogue.

AK: My poems are in my mind and they come to me like scenes in a movie; there isn't necessarily any sequence to them—they're more like a series of disconnected individual scenes. And I use them in my imagination, but not in the dialogue of the movie.

JR: When did you start writing these poems?

AK: I can't remember, but perhaps twenty years ago. (*He reads aloud.*) "A white foal / emerges through the fog / and disappears / into the fog." They usually focus on a single moment. Or an encounter: "Angry confrontation between two prostitutes / leaving the church / on Sunday afternoon."

JR: My favorite of your short films is *Orderly or Disorderly* [1981], and I'm wondering how that film developed.

AK: When I was working for the Center for the Intellectual Development of Children and Young Adults [Kanun], there was no boss to put pressure on us to make a certain type of film. But we noticed that most films then weren't suitable for children, so we decided to make educational films about the social relationships of children. I found a Canadian film catalog containing descriptions of over fourteen hundred educational films, including some by Norman McLaren, and I used that as a starting point for thinking up ideas for films of my own. One idea I had was to show children why it was important to drive well, what was wrong about driving badly, or to show them why it was important to brush their teeth. Why, when you're half asleep, do you have to put this awful-tasting stuff on your toothbrush and then place it in your mouth? Because of the ways that rules of this kind often aren't observed in Iran, one could say that this film is the beginning of a series of works that show why order is better than disorder.

Two Solutions for One Problem [1975] essentially grew out of the same idea, which is also the same idea as the "Dialogue between Civilizations," the first big seminar held with international filmmakers at the Fajr Film Festival this year. This was suggested twenty-five years ago when we said that the solution to disagreements was to have a dialogue. Incidentally, I wasn't thinking then about creating art movies or something poetic. But since they were addressed to children and I had to use simple language, these films found forms that responded to and were appropriate to their contents. Since the goal was clear and the language was simple, the form that was created became artistic.

JR: It's also interesting to me that there's an ambiguous relation between fiction and documentary in this film that recurs in your subsequent work. When you hear the camera crew give an aesthetic critique of the way a shot plays out, while filming the way kids board a bus in an orderly or disorderly fashion, it's not clear to what extent this is a documentary or a satire about how filmmakers behave. In fact, it's rather like the opening sequence of *The Wind Will Carry Us;* the offscreen comments are similar in a way, and equally funny.

AK: I personally can't define the difference between a documentary and a narrative film. For instance, *Close-up,* a movie that's based on a true story, with the real characters in the real locations, would seem to qualify as a documentary. But because it restages everything, it isn't a documentary, so I don't know which drawer to put it in. You know, even a photograph can tell a story, and the very fact that you've picked one scene and omitted other scenes, or selected one lens over another lens, shows that you've done something special and told a story with that photograph; you're intervening in reality. One day when I was wondering, What exactly *is* a documentary, as opposed to the other kinds of movies that we make? I finally decided that if you just attach the camera to the top of a bull's horns and let him loose in a field for a whole day, at the end of the day you might have a documentary. But there's still a catch here, because we've selected the location and the type of lens that we want.

JR: And the kind of bull.

AK: And whether it's a cloudy day or a sunny day. In my mind, there isn't as much of a distinction between documentary and fiction as there is between a good movie and a bad one.

MS: I'm curious to know if your early experiences making commercials and designing credit sequences had any effect on your later films. I recently saw one of those credit sequences and thought that its design was very characteristic of your work.

AK: You might say that my period in advertising had no impact on my later films. But then again, if you look closely you will find relationships and influences. As far as the credit sequences are concerned, someone told me that the first scene in my last movie [*The Wind Will Carry Us*] duplicated a scene in my first movie. I said it actually started with the zigzagging path in *Where Is the Friend's House?* but my friend pointed out that in my very first film, *Bread and Alley,* if you look at the alley from an overhead angle, the alley where the boy is running is also zigzagging. In fact, I believe this image was always in my mind but turned up in the films unconsciously. So you can probably find traces of my old advertising films in my new films as well—but not conscious traces.

JR: I'm wondering if you ever had much interest in comic strips. The way you use offscreen dialogue over long shots of cars reminds me of some of them.

AK: Truthfully, I don't recall reading them much or caring for them.

MS: There seems to be a progressive movement in your films away from narrative. Is this a development that you're conscious of? In *Report* [1977], everything seems much more tied to a specific story.

AK: (*in English*) That one belongs to that time. Not a revolution outside but a revolution inside myself, because I was married at that time and had the same problem [as my hero]. I was always inside—the camera was inside—so it's totally different.

MS: And you worked with professional actors?

AK: (*in English*) No, I did not. She [Shohreh Aghdashlu] was not—it was her first film—and Kurosh [Afsharpanah] wasn't either. Nobody was.

MS: Would it be accurate to say that *Report* was very close to what was happening in Iran at the time, unlike many of your later films?

AK: (*in English*) Yes, but this happened by itself. Not consciously. Because I didn't want to change my job or my role. If you're interested in what happened between *Report* and my more recent films, for me it's that I changed my mind about life. I'm not inside my home as much as before; I don't have the same problems. I've worked with children, so I'm much closer to children now, and I'm much closer to nature and to landscapes. I wasn't a photographer then, but I'm a photographer now. So many, many things have changed in my personal life. I live in my home. Before, my household consisted of four persons. Now I'm alone, living by myself. So any period will change something in your way, your style, your cinema, and your vision of life.

JR: One thing I found interesting that was uncharacteristic in *Case No. 1, Case No. 2* [1979] is that the film's form is very aggressive, yet it finally seems like an afterthought—or, more precisely, like a pretext, having little to do with what the film is actually about. The situation whereby students either report on one another or take a mutual vow of silence, posing an issue to all the adults interviewed, certainly gets them talking. But the second half of the film doesn't generate responses from them that are noticeably different from those in the first part.

AK: The first part was really a game—an excuse for the rest to happen and for people to talk. There's a kind of math problem in school where the first part is irrelevant to the second part, but still you use it in order to make a point. You start out with a man who wants to sell fifty oranges, and then you suddenly ask what color his shirt is. So the story that concentrates on children ends here so the adults can get their messages across. And my conversations with these people made it more obvious to me that those who were illiterate and who didn't have much understanding of social life do need or require some kind of government or governing body to dictate to them what to do and how to live—because they're unable to decide for themselves what is right and wrong.

May 2001, Faxes in Persian between Chicago and Tehran

JR: Do you see *A.B.C. Africa* as part of your overall project to use the audience's imagination and collaboration? It's striking how important scenes in darkness are in your last two films. Do you think they function at all similarly?

AK: Yes, but this wasn't a preplanned goal. After a few days in Africa, I realized that my concept of the country, which I got from TV, was very different from what I saw. [From TV] I knew an Africa that in the depths of ugliness, sickness, and filth was in the process of dying, and from that vantage point AIDS looked like a blessing that could end this tragedy as quickly as possible. But my concept of Africa was altered during the first few days. I even found the people beautiful, and the place as well—primitive but also civilized. An incredible contrast: very poor from the outside but rich from the inside and very much interested in life, an image that I believe is apparent in the film.

The function of darkness in the two films is identical, but in each case it has its own rationale. For me, light and image can only be meaningful in relation to this darkness. We're accustomed to images, images that are constantly in front of our eyes. Even our language tends to work with images, and naturally in the course of this visual bombardment the meaning of images is completely forgotten. I think the image recovers its meaning when it faces darkness, just as light does. In the darkness we arrive at an image through sound—an image which is based on our own experience and which therefore differs with each viewer. Every viewer creates his own image with his imagination, and this is exactly what I want, my ideal situation; the audience participates in the film's creative mise en scène. The ideal of darkness in *A.B.C. Africa* takes its form from the reality of living in darkness in Africa, without electricity, and the rainy morning after the painful seven minutes in the dark is a gift to those who have patiently tolerated the dark night until the morning.

MS: Did you restage certain scenes, such as the ones in the darkness and in the ruins? How many of the locations were scouted in advance?

AK: We didn't restage anything in this film—we didn't have the time—but the two cameras being in the right place at the right time gave us this opportunity to bring a kind of mise en scène to the film at certain moments. We were seeing all those locations for the first time; we planned to visit the hospital and we were supposed to stay there twenty minutes. So the death of the child and wrapping his body on the back of the bicycle was completely accidental and unplanned.

JR: Did you conceptualize different roles for the two cameras? I noticed that Seiffollah Samadian's camera was much larger than yours.

AK: No, these were the cameras we happened to have with us. In other films as well, when scouting locations and working on the script, I had a digital video camera that I used just like a drafting pen. On this trip Seiffollah brought his own camera, which was a little more sophisticated than mine. Of course, our original intention was not to make the film on this trip. As was suggested in the invitation, the plan was to see the place so that I could make the film later according to IFAD's [the International Fund of Agricultural Development's] wishes. But our felt tip and fine point drafting pens wound up taking enough notes to make a film. I believe that a restaged film based on an original plan is never as good. So we just edited what we had. My camera wasn't perfect, but I thought it was good enough for this kind of film, which revolves around the subject matter.

MS: Was this the first time you've allowed someone else to decide on certain camera angles?

AK: No, it wasn't the first time. In every film where the camera is controlled by the cameraman, the selection and the coordination of the elements within the frame in relation to the film's subject is up to him. How close the filmmaker and cinematographer get to treating the subject the same way determines how much the mise en scène becomes a united effort or at least how much it approaches that ideal.

JR: What do you think of the thirty-five millimeter transfer, assuming that you've been able to see it yet? (We haven't.)

AK: I think that in order to transfer DV to thiry-five millimeter, one has to respect the mise en scène that works for DV. The fast pans often created a problem when making the transfer. To use these cameras, one also has to be careful with the set design and the costume design. White and bright colors create problems. For close-ups, this camera is fantastic. The most important advantage is that it doesn't need complicated and difficult lighting, so you need fewer crew members around the people you're shooting—especially the nonprofessional actors, for whom the presence of cameras is always a nuisance. The small size of this camera can quickly be forgotten by them, and more sensitive scenes involving feelings between the directors and actors can be created as a consequence. So we can arrive that way at acting that is more real and simpler. Static shots at night using available light are one of the most important things this camera can handle. I think filmmaking in the style of Bresson is a wonderful idea for this kind of camera.

JR: *A.B.C. Africa* begins with a few people arriving in Uganda and ends with a few people leaving. Is it your desire for the audience to forget the presence of the filmmakers in the final scenes?

AK: This was a framework to shape the film. The arrival of the filmmakers in Uganda was based on the reality. And the ending, the immigration of the child who is uprooted from her land to an unknown place, was taken from an idea—the idea that this could perhaps turn out to be a crude and unwise solution. Maybe this sort of ending is not defensible as a solution. Somewhere in the film it's said that we're trying to keep these children with their families, homes, and communities: we don't want to separate them from their native land. So the film's resolution is not a defensible solution, but it wraps up the film. I trust the viewer's feelings, knowledge, and sense of judgment in this matter. If this resolution is a wrong one, then what is the right one? Does adopting a child reduce the feelings of guilt that we probably have about the destinies of millions of orphans throughout Africa? Have we really played some part on our own in creating this tragedy? Relying on the scrutinizing look of the audience, which I believe is thoughtful and knowledgeable, I give myself permission to make a mistake.

JR: Have the members of the UWESO [Uganda Women's Efforts to Save Orphans] or the IFAD seen *A.B.C. Africa* yet? If so, what do they think?

AK: Yes, they've seen it and their reactions have been very positive. The executive who invited me said something to me that surprised me. He said, "Take out the scenes that make it look like a commissioned film," and that's what we did. He believed that the film could be more impressive without an imposed agenda. Contrary to what I expected, he thought the film wasn't like other commissioned films and was effective for just that reason.

MS: Have you received other requests to make films about social problems? If that's the case, why did you decide to make this one?

AK: I haven't received an invitation like this one before. *Homework* and some short films like *Fellow Citizen* [1983] or *Tribute to the Teachers* [1977] had themes of social issues and problems that led me to accept them as self-commissioned works. The subject of this film attracted me for certain other reasons: so I could go at a good time of year (springtime), visit a continent I hadn't been to before (Africa), work on an original and ambiguous subject (AIDS), and return to the world of children.

JR: There are obviously important differences between the sound we heard in the version of *A.B.C. Africa* shown in Tehran and the final mix, and the ones I'm most aware of are the changes in the music—some of which I believe came in part from problems with clearing music rights. Although in some ways I regret the loss of "Autumn Leaves" in the scene at the ruins (which for me is the most beautiful scene in the film—certainly the most lyrical), mainly because I love this song, the faint guitar one hears is certainly much more subtle. Similarly, in the last scene you've substituted the sounds of the plane and an even more faint version of the "Blue Danube" waltz for baroque music that I believe was by Handel. The baroque music for me signified western Europe, while the Strauss waltz makes me think of eastern Europe, Vienna in particular. One overall difference in both these changes is that it makes the African music seem much more dominant and central. Was this part of your intention?

AK: I agree with you that in the presence of African music, the classical music did not have the same effectiveness. The native music has a genuine indigenous quality—meaning that classical music, which I am very fond of and can never call either Western or Eastern, doesn't have that quality. For me classical music belongs to everywhere and everyone and, just like the sky, has no nationality or geography. But I thought it was a little too chic and fancy to be used in this film, so the ending music changed a little bit in the final version that you haven't seen yet. The "Blue Danube" waltz was more appropriate for the ending than the music you heard in Tehran—a piece by Haydn which was too heavy for this film. Although the "Blue Danube" was more suitable for this film, I also found it intrusive. So I lowered the volume bit by bit and then eventually I removed it. In the thirty-five millimeter print, the film ends only with the sounds of the airplane.

Regarding the changes of the other pieces in the film, some were due to copyright and some were because I wasn't sure if they were the best choices, so eventually we took them out. "Autumn Leaves" was one such case. It was a pleasant piece outside the film and wasn't bad in the film, but it triggered something in the mind of viewers that had nothing to do with the film's subject. So for this reason, when I noticed in private screenings that viewers were whispering to one another, the fact that they knew the piece made it unsuitable, so I wound up using another piece instead. The selection of the new piece had something to do with wanting a sound more than a song. The music you hear played on the guitar is written by a young Iranian composer and I wanted to place it somewhere in the film. The young man is the boy who hid behind a narrow tree to take a pee in *Life and Nothing More . . .* [1992].

MS: Have you stayed in touch with some of the people you filmed, including the Austrian couple? Do you know what's happened to them? Would you like to shoot in Africa again?

AK: I haven't been in touch with the couple—not yet. I have their address, and MK2 [Productions] is going to send them a copy of the film. Do you remember the interview with the Austrian parents in the car? When the father was telling his baby in a teasing tone, "Do you want to say something in baby language?" and the baby just put the microphone against her cheeks? I hope I'll have the opportunity to ask her many years from now, maybe in twenty years, if she is happy with her white parents away from her country, thanks to having immigrated.

More than returning to Africa as a filmmaker, I'd like to go there again as a photographer, go to remote places where cameras have never been—where they don't know the camera and they stand in front of it as much as you like and stare at it without changing their position. Since they have no idea they're being recorded and don't know about photographs, that gives me the opportunity to change my angle several times, change my lenses, and take their photograph in a completely relaxed atmosphere that professionals would call spontaneous.

Statement on *10*

The following ten paragraphs written by Abbas Kiarostami, printed here verbatim, were published in the press book for *10* when the film premiered at the Cannes Film Festival in May 2002.

Sometimes, I tell myself that *10* is a film I could never make again. You cannot decide to make such a film. . . . It's a little like *Close-up*. It's possible to continue along the same path but it requires a great deal of patience. Indeed, this is not something that can be repeated easily. It must occur of its own accord, like an incident or a happening. . . . At the same time, it requires a great deal of preparation. Originally, this was the story of a psychoanalyst, her patients and her car, but that was two years ago. . . .

I was invited to Beirut in Lebanon last week, for a film workshop with students. One of them told me, "You're the only one who can make such a film because of your reputation. If one of us had made it, no one would have accepted it." I replied that, as his teacher, I owed him the truth: making something simple requires a great deal of experience. And, first of all, you need to understand that simplicity isn't the same as facility.

Kundera tells a fascinating story that genuinely impressed me: he relates how his father's lexical range diminished with age and, at the end of his life, was reduced to two words: "It's strange! It's strange!" Of course, he hadn't reached that point because he had nothing much to say anymore but because those two words effectively summed up his life's experience. They were the very essence of it. Perhaps that's the story behind minimalism too. . . .

The disappearance of direction. That's what is at stake: the rejection of all elements vital to ordinary cinema. I state, with a great deal of caution, that direction, in the usual sense of the word, can vanish in this kind of process. In this form of cinema, the director is more like a football coach. He has to do most of his work before the take starts. Indeed, for me, the film always starts well before the initial preparation and is almost never over. It's a never-ending game. Each time I show it, I await the audience's reactions. The discussions following the screening take a new turn each time. . . . For me, the beauty of art resides in the reactions that it causes.

This film was created without being made as such. Even so, it isn't a documentary. Neither a documentary nor a purely fabricated film. Midway between the two perhaps. . . . A scene occurs and I decide that it suits me. Later, I realize that one particular element was vital for the integration of the whole.

In *10*, we have a shot in the car with the little boy facing the camera. The scene takes place in front of the camera. And yet there are also people who pass by, lower their window, and peer into the car. That's documentary. That's background. They look at the camera. But what happens in front of the camera isn't documentary because it's guided and controlled in a way. The person in front of the camera manages to forget its presence, it vanishes for him. Emotion is created in this way, the result of a certain quantity of energy and information that we give and then recover later. It circulates . . . resulting in the complexity of the situation. This flow must be controlled in order to be released at the right moment.

You cannot promise yourself that you'll make another film like this. It's like wavering in your staunchest convictions and ideas. Sometimes it's easier to protect yourself with good old direction, the scenery, the set. . . .

If anyone were to ask me what I did as a director on the film, I'd say, "Nothing and yet if I didn't exist, this film wouldn't have existed."

In all my films, there are shots where the emotional impact goes beyond direction, triumphing over it, and the emotion becomes more powerful than cinema itself. There's the shot in *Taste of Cherry* where Mr. Badii, while talking about himself, refuses to let out his emotion. And the corners of his mouth start trembling as he begins to sob. These are shots that I do not claim to have created. They deserve better than that. I was able to provoke them and seize them at the right moment. That's all.

This film is my own "two words". It sums up almost everything. I say "almost" because I'm already thinking about my next film. A one-word film perhaps.

Filmography

Kiarostami makes commercials (1962–66) and title credits for films (e.g., Mohammad Zarrindast's *Satan's Temptation* [1967], Masud Kimiae's *Ghaysar* [1969] and *Reza Motori* [1970]; and Jalal Maghedam's *The Window* [1970]).

Bread and Alley (*Nan-O Kucheh;* 1970; short)
Production: Kanun
Director: Abbas Kiarostami
Screenplay: Taghi Kiarostami, brother of Abbas
Photography: Mehrdad Fakhimi
Editing: Manuchehr Oliai
Sound: Harayer Ateshkar
Music: Paul Desmond (?) playing "Ob-La-Di, Ob-La-Da"
Cast: Reza Hashemi (boy), Mehdi Shahvenfar (old man)
Black and white
35 mm
10 minutes, 45 seconds
On his way home from buying bread, a small boy encounters a stray dog who barks at him.

Recess (*Zang-e Tafrih;* 1972; short)
Production: Kanun
Director: Abbas Kiarostami
Screenplay: Abbas Kiarostami, based on a story by Masud Madani
Photography: Ali-Reza Zarrindast, Morteza Rastegar
Editing: Rouhollah Emami
Sound: Harayer Ateshkar
Cast: Cyrus Hassanpour
Black and white
35 mm
14 minutes, 45 seconds
A boy walks home from school after being ejected from class for breaking a window.

The Experience (*Tajrobeh;* 1973; short feature)
Production: Kanun
Direction: Abbas Kiarostami
Screenplay: Abbas Kiarostami, based on a story by Amir Naderi
Photography: Ali-Reza Zarrindast
Editing: Mehdi Rejaian
Cast: Hassan Yar-Mohamadi, Parviz Naderi, Andre Guvalovich
Black and white
35 mm
60 minutes
Mamad, a fourteen-year-old boy who runs errands at a photography shop, pines for a young middle-class girl and tries unsuccessfully to get a job at her home.

Jahan Nama Palace (*Ghasr-e Jahan Nama;* 1974; documentary short)
Direction: Abbas Kiarostami
Photography: Firuz Malekzadeh
Sound: Tehengir Azad, Changiz Sayad
Narration: Monouchehr Anvar
Color
16 mm
31 minutes
A commissioned work about the restoration of the title palace

The Traveler (*Mosafer;* 1974; short feature)
Production: Kanun
Direction: Abbas Kiarostami
Screenplay: Abbas Kiarostami, based on a story by Hassan Rafie
Photography: Firuz Malekzadeh
Editing: Amir-Hossein Hesami
Music: Kambiz Rushanavan
Cast: Hasan Darabi (Qasem), Massud Zand Pegleh, Mostafa Tari
Black and white
35 mm
71 minutes, 25 seconds
When he hears that his favorite soccer team will be playing in Tehran, Qasem schemes to raise the money for a bus ticket but then falls asleep and dreams just before the big game, waking to find the stadium already deserted.

Two Solutions for One Problem (*Do Rah-e Hal Baray-e Yek Masaleh;* 1975; short)
Production: Kanun
Direction: Abbas Kiarostami with Assistant Director M. Haji
Screenplay: Abbas Kiarostami
Photography: Morteza Rastegar

Editing: Abbas Kiarostami
Sound: Changiz Sayad
Color
35 mm
4 minutes, 25 seconds
Two friends at school, Dara and Nader, get into an extended grudge match after Dara returns Nader's textbook with its cover torn. After totaling the damage, the adult male narrator proposes a friendlier solution.

So Can I (*Manam Mitunam;* 1975; short)
Production: Kanun
Direction: Abbas Kiarostami
Screenplay: Abbas Kiarostami
Photography: Mostafa Haji
Editing: Abbas Kiarostami
Sound: Harayer Ateshkar, M. Haqiqi
Music: Nasser Cheshmazar
Animation: Farzaneh Taghavi
Cast: Kamal Riahi, Ahmad Kiarostami
Color
35 mm
3 minutes, 30 seconds
Two children watching animals move in an animated film try to imitate their gestures—until they see real birds fly and a real airplane take off.

The Colors (*Rangha;* 1975; short)
Production: Kanun
Direction: Abbas Kiarostami
Screenplay: Abbas Kiarostami
Photography: Morteza Rastegar, Mostafa Haji
Editing: Abbas Kiarostami
Sound: Changiz Sayad
Cast: Shahin Amir-Arjomand
Color
35 mm
15 minutes
Brief didactic lessons about colors and related matters

The Wedding Suit (*Lebasi Baray-e Arusi;* 1976; short feature)
Production: Kanun, Ebrahim Foruzesh
Direction: Abbas Kiarostami with Assistant Director Ahmad Mirshekari
Screenplay: Abbas Kiarostami with Parviz Davai
Photography: Firuz Malekzadeh

Editing: Mousa Afshar
Cast: Mohammad Fazih Motaleb, Massud Zand Begleh, Mehdi Nekui
Color
35 mm
57 minutes
Ali, a boy who works in a tailor's shop, lends a new wedding suit made for a customer to a friend who works in the same building.

How We Should Use Our Free Time (*Az Oghat-e Faaghat-e Khod Cheguneh Estefadeh Konim;* 1977; short)
Direction: Abbas Kiarostami
7 minutes
(This short may be lost.)

Report (*Gozaresh;* 1977; feature)
Production: Bahman Farmanara
Direction: Abbas Kiarostami
Screenplay: Abbas Kiarostami
Photography: Ali-Reza Zarindast
Editing: Mah-Talaat Mirfendereski
Sound: Yusef Shahab
Cast: Shohreh Agdashlu (wife), Kurosh Afsharpanah (Mohammad), Mostafa Tari
Color
35 mm
112 minutes
Mohammad Firuzkuhi, a tax auditor at the Ministry of Finance, is accused of graft relating to one of his old cases; meanwhile, his rent is overdue and his wife berates him while they shop. Back at home, he beats her and leaves with their child. After discovering that she attempted suicide, he takes her to the hospital but leaves alone after discovering that she will live.

Tribute to the Teachers (*Bozorgdasht-e Moallem;* 1977; short)
Direction: Abbas Kiarostami
20 minutes
The comments and complaints of teachers about educational issues and teacher-student relations
(This short may be lost.)

Solution (*Rah-e Hal;* 1978; short)
Production: Kanun
Direction: Abbas Kiarostami
Screenplay: Abbas Kiarostami
Photography: Firuz Malekzadeh

Editing: Abbas Kiarostami
Sound: Changiz Sayad
Color
16 mm
11 minutes, 55 seconds
On a wintry mountain road, a man carrying a spare tire decides to roll it toward his car, parked some distance away.

Case No. 1, Case No. 2 (*Qazih-e Shekl-e Aval, Dovom;* 1979; documentary feature)
Production: Kanun
Direction: Abbas Kiarostami with Assistant Director Naser Zera'ati
Photography: Baharalu
Editing: Abbas Kiarostami
Sound: Changiz Sayad
Color
16 mm
53 minutes
A professor expels seven male students when no one confesses to making a disturbance while his back is turned. Kiarostami asks several adults—all of them representing moral authority (politicians, religious leaders or devotees, intellectuals, media people, parents)—whether they approve of this silence. After one student fingers the guilty party, the adults are interviewed about this response to the problem.

Toothache (*Dandan-e Dard;* 1980; short)
Production: Kanun
Direction: Abbas Kiarostami
Photography: Firuz Malekzadeh
Sound: Changiz Sayad
Color
16 mm
24 minutes
Lessons in dental hygiene

The Driver (*Ranandeh;* 1980; feature)
Direction: Naser Zara'ati
Screenplay: Abbas Kiarostami
Editing: Abbas Kiarostami

Orderly or Disorderly (*Be Tartib Ya Bedun-e Tartib;* 1981; short)
Production: Kanun
Direction: Abbas Kiarostami

Screenplay: Abbas Kiarostami
Sound: Changiz Sayad
Color
35 mm
15 minutes
In separate takes, Kiarostami films the orderly and disorderly behavior of children at school—leaving class, going to a water fountain, boarding a bus—while he talks with his crew about some of the aesthetic qualities of each camera setup. Then he films orderly and disorderly traffic at a busy intersection.

The Chorus (*Hamsorayan;* 1982; short)
Production: Kanun
Direction: Abbas Kiarostami with Assistant Director Naser Zera'ati
Screenplay: Abbas Kiarostami, based on a story by Mohammad Javad Kahnamoie
Photography: A. R. Zarindast
Editing: Abbas Kiarostami
Sound: Ahmad Asgari, Changiz Sayad
Cast: Yusef Moqaddam, Ali Asgari, Teymur and other children from Rasht
Color
35 mm
17 minutes
An old man in Rasht turns off his hearing aid when street sounds become too grating, so he can't hear his granddaughter when she rings his doorbell.

Fellow Citizen (*Hamshahri;* 1983; short documentary feature)
Production: Kanun
Direction: Abbas Kiarostami
Screenplay: Abbas Kiarostami
Photography: Firuz Malekzadeh
Sound: M. Haqiqi
Cast: Reza Mansuri (traffic cop)
Color
16 mm
53 minutes
The everyday life of a traffic cop in Tehran

Fear and Suspicion (*Tars Va Su-e Zan;* 1984; television series)
Direction: Abbas Kiarostami
Thirteen episodes were planned; one or two were filmed, but none was ever broadcast.
Kiarostami and a psychologist screen clips from Kiarostami's films and poll twenty or so spectators regarding their responses.
(This series may be lost.)

The Look (*Negah;* 1984; short)
Direction: Ebrahim Furuzesh
Editing: Abbas Kiarostami

Class Bell, Recess Bell (*Zang-e Dars, Zang-e Tafrih;* 1984) (short)
Direction: Iraj Karimi
Editing: Abbas Kiarostami

First Graders (*Avaliha;* 1984; documentary feature)
Production: Kanun
Direction: Abbas Kiarostami
Screenplay: Abbas Kiarostami
Photography: Homayun Payvar
Editing: Abbas Kiarostami
Sound: Changiz Sayad
Cast: teachers, staff, and pupils at the Tohid School
Color
16 mm
85 minutes
A look at the everyday operations of a grammar school in a poor neighborhood

The Moments (*Lahzeh-ha;* 1985; short)
Direction: Iraj Karimi
Editing: Abbas Kiarostami

I, Myself (*Khodam, Man Khodam;* 1985; feature)
Direction: Ebrahim Furuzesh
Screenplay: Abbas Kiarostami
Editing: Abbas Kiarostami

The Key (*Kelid;* 1986; feature)
Direction: Ebrahim Furuzesh
Screenplay: Abbas Kiarostami
Editing: Abbas Kiarostami
72 minutes
A story about a little boy locked in his home

Where Is the Friend's House? (*Khaneh-ye Dust Kojast?* 1986; feature)
Production: Kanun, Ali-Reza Zarrin
Direction: Abbas Kiarostami
Screenplay: Abbas Kiarostami
Editing: Abbas Kiarostami
Photography: Farhad Saba
Cast: Babak Ahmadpour, Ahmad Ahmadpour

Color
35 mm
92 minutes
A young pupil, Mohammad-Reza Nematzadeh, is reprimanded by his teacher for not doing his homework and is threatened with expulsion if he fails to do another assignment. His classmate Ahmad, who lives in a neighboring village, accidentally brings his friend's notebook home and searches for him so that he can return it. He gives up his search by nightfall but the next morning returns the notebook with the homework done.

Homework (*Mashgh-e Shab;* 1988; documentary feature)
Production: Kanun, Ali-Reza Zarrin
Direction: Abbas Kiarostami
Screenplay: Abbas Kiarostami
Photography: Iraj Safavi, Ali Asghar Mirza
Editing: Abbas Kiarostami
Music: Mohammad-Reza Aligholi
Research: Saeed Dolatabadi
Color
16 mm
86 minutes
Investigative journalism about children's homework and the abuse of children, addressed through Kiarostami's interviews with the children and a few parents

The Three Faces of a School Proctor (*Seh Chehreh az Yek Mobser;* 1989; short)
Direction: Hassan Aqa Karimi
Screenplay: Abbas Kiarostami

The Wild Irises (*Zanbaqa-haye Vashi;* 1989; short)
Direction: Ebrahim Furuzesh
Editing: Abbas Kiarostami

Close-up (*Namay-e Nazdik;* 1990; docudrama feature)
Production: Kanun, Ali-Reza Zarrin
Director: Abbas Kiarostami
Screenplay: Abbas Kiarostami
Photography: Ali-Reza Zarrindast
Editing: Abbas Kiarostami
Music: Kambiz Roushanavan (theme from *The Traveler*)
Cast: Hossein Sabzian (imposter), Mehrdad Ahankhah (imposter's victim), Houshang Shamai, Mohsen Makhmalbaf (director), Hassan Farazmand (reporter)
Color

35 mm
102 minutes
Hassan Farazmand, a reporter at *Soroush* magazine, goes with the police to the home of the Ahankhah family to arrest Hossain Sabzian for impersonating the filmmaker Mohsen Makhmalbaf on the pretext of preparing a film with the family. Kiarostami visits Sabzian in jail and gets permission to make a film about the case, including the trial, at which the court eventually acquits Sabzian. The day he's freed from jail, the real Makhmalbaf comes to meet Sabzian, and together they ride Makhmalbaf's motorbike to the Ahankhahs' home to apologize to the family.

Life and Nothing More . . . (*. . . Va Zendengi Edameh Darad;* 1992; feature)
Production: Kanun, Ali-Reza Zarrin
Direction: Abbas Kiarostami
Screenplay: Abbas Kiarostami
Photography: Homayoun Pievar
Editing: Abbas Kiarostami
Sound: Changiz Sayad
Music: Vivaldi
Cast: Farhad Kheradmand (director) Puya Pievar (his son), Hossein Rezai (villager who wants to get married), inhabitants of Rudbar and Rostamabad
Color
35 mm
91 minutes
Three days after a severe earthquake in northern Iran in June 1990, a director and his son set out to find Ahmad Ahmadpour and Babak Ahmadpour, lead actors in the father's film *Where Is the Friend's House?* in a village in the area. Because the main road is congested with traffic, the two have to travel by side roads, and they eventually hear that the boys are alive without ever seeing them. The father and son talk to many survivors over the course of the day and give a ride to a boy looking forward to watching a soccer match on television.

Through the Olive Trees (*Zir-e Derakhtan-e Zeytun;* 1994; feature)
Production: Abbas Kiarostami
Direction: Abbas Kiarostami with Assistant Director Jafar Panahi
Screenplay: Abbas Kiarostami
Photography: Hossein Jafarian with Farhad Saba, Bahram Badakhshani, Farzad Jodat
Editing: Abbas Kiarostami
Sound: Mahmud Samakbashi
Cast: Mohammad-Ali Keshavarz (director), Farhad Kheradmand (crew member), Hossein Rezai (young actor), Tahereh Ladanian (young actress)

Color
35 mm
103 minutes
Keshavarz, a filmmaker, has chosen two local nonprofessionals to reenact a scene from *Life and Nothing More*. . . . But the young man flubs his lines every time he addresses the woman and the filmmaker then asks Hossein, a gofer on the production, to take over the role. Initially the young woman, Tahereh, refuses to work with the impoverished Hossein, who has been courting her for a long time without success, but she finally agrees to appear in the film with him. Hossein uses the occasion to propose to her again, though she refuses to speak to him when they aren't working. At the end of the film, she runs across a field of olive trees and, at Keshavarz's suggestion, Hossein follows her (while Keshavarz follows Hossein). From a distance, we see that after Hossein catches up with her, he turns and runs away.

The White Balloon (*Badkonak-e sefid;* 1995; feature)
Direction: Jafar Panahi
Screenplay: Abbas Kiarostami
84 minutes

The Journey (*Safar;* 1995; feature)
Direction: Ali-Reza Raisian
Screenplay: Abbas Kiarostami

Réparages, in *A propos de Nice, la suite* (1995; feature of sketches)
Production: La Sept Cinema/New Age Productions (France)
Direction: Abbas Kiarostami with Parviz Kimiavi
Screenplay: Abbas Kiarostami
Photography: Jacques Bouquin
Editing: Anne Belin
Sound: Jean-Pierre Fenie
Cast: Christine Heinrich-Burelt (taxi driver), Parviz Kimiavi (filmmaker), Simone Lecorre (bar customer), Luce Vigo (herself)
Color
35 mm
105 minutes
Each sketch in *A propos de Nice, la suite* is inspired by Jean Vigo's 1930 experimental documentary about Nice. In *Réparages,* a foreign filmmaker comes to Nice to look for tangible and spiritual traces of Vigo and instead finds one of Vigo's extras. The directors and writers of the other episodes are Catherine Breillat, Costa-Gavras, Clare Denis, Raymond Depardon, Jean-Marie G. Le Clézio, Pavel Lounguine, and Raùl Ruiz.

Lumière and Company (1996; feature composed of short segments)
Production: Lumière Company
Direction: Abbas Kiarostami
Screenplay: Abbas Kiarostami
Photography: Philippe Poulet
Editing: Abbas Kiarostami
Voice: Isabelle Huppert
Color
35 mm
52 seconds
To commemorate the centennial of the Lumière brothers' first motion pictures, about forty international filmmakers, including Kiarostami, created their own fifty-two-second films using the Lumières' restored original camera. Kiarostami's segment was made in Locarno in August 1995 during the Locarno International Film Festival.
A man's hand breaks an egg into a frying pan and the egg cooks while a woman's voice is heard off-screen on an answering machine, inviting him to dinner. The hand takes the pan away from the stove.

Birth of Light (*Tavalod-e Nur;* 1997; short)
Production: Waka Films
Direction: Abbas Kiarostami
5 minutes
A thin ray of light penetrates the darkness of a starry sky. The sun rises, shining from behind the mountain.

Taste of Cherry (*Tam-e Gilas;* 1997; feature)
Production: Abbas Kiarostami
Direction: Abbas Kiarostami
Photography: Homayoun Pievar
Editing: Abbas Kiarostami
Cast: Homayoun Ershadi (Mr. Badii), Safir Ali Moradi (the soldier), Mir Hossain Noori (the seminarian), Abdolhossein Bagheri (the Turkish taxidermist), Afhshin Khorshid Bakhtari. Music: Louis Armstrong, "St. James Infirmary" (trumpet solo only)
Color
35 mm
99 minutes
A middle-aged man named Mr. Badii searches the city's dry, barren outskirts in his car to find someone to bury him after he commits suicide or to retrieve him if his effort fails. He gives rides to a soldier and to an Afghani religious student, both of whom refuse his cash offer. Finally he encounters an old Turkish taxidermist named Bagheri, an employee of a wildlife museum who

agrees reluctantly. Badii goes home, and that night during stormy weather, he takes a taxi to the grave, lies in it, and waits for death. The film switches to video, and it is now daytime with the trees in bloom. Kiarostami, his crew, and the actor who plays Badii are seen filming a group of soldiers marching on the field beside the grave; at the director's request, everyone stops work and rests.

Willow and Wind (*Bid o bad;* 1999; feature)
Direction: Mohammad Ali Talebi
Screenplay: Abbas Kiarostami

The Wind Will Carry Us (. . . *Baad Mara Khahad Bord;* 1999; feature)
Production: Abbas Kiarostami with Marin Karmitz (MK2 Productions)
Direction: Abbas Kiarostami with Assistant Director Bahman Ghobadi
Screenplay: Based on a story by Mahmud Aidin
Photography: Mahoud Kalari
Editing: Abbas Kiarostami
Sound Recordist: Jahangir Mirshekari
Sound Mixer: Mohammad-Reza Delpak
Music: Peyman Yazdanian
Cast: Behzad Dorani (Behzad) and the inhabitants of a Kurdish village
Color
35 mm
118 minutes
A few people arrive by car from Tehran for a short stay at Siah Dareh, a village in Iranian Kurdistan. The locals do not know why the visitors have come (a false rumor is circulated about hunting for treasure), but it soon becomes clear that they're awaiting the death of a one hundred-year-old woman so that they can film a self-mutilation ritual carried out by some of the local women at funerals. The apparent leader of the group—whom the locals call an engineer and who befriends the old woman's grandson, a schoolboy, to hear about her condition and what's happening in the village—periodically drives to the top of a hill, the site of a former cemetery, whenever he receives calls on his cellular phone. There he also converses with a man digging a deep hole "for communications purposes." After flirting with this man's fiancée in the village while she milks a cow, he rushes to alert the villagers when the digger is buried under a cave-in, and they manage to save him before he suffocates. Returning from the hospital where the digger is taken by a doctor, the group's leader discovers that the old woman has died but that his companions from Tehran have already left.
After winning the Special Jury Prize as well as the FIPRESCI prize for *The Wind Will Carry Us* at the 56th Venice International Film Festival, Kiarostami announces that he will no longer submit any of his films in competition at film

festivals, having received enough prizes by this time. (Prior to these prizes, according to a list compiled by the critic Mohammad Atebbai, Kiarostami had received a total of forty-six film festival prizes since 1970.)

A.B.C. Africa (2001; documentary feature)
Direction: Abbas Kiarostami with Assistant Director Seiffollah Samadian
Photography: Abbas Kiarostami with Seiffollah Samadian
Editing: Abbas Kiarostami with Seiffollah Samadian
Music: guitar played by Puya Pievar and Ugandan music
Color
Digital video transferred to 35 mm
84 minutes
Kiarostami receives a fax from Takeo Shibata requesting that he make a documentary about the children orphaned by victims of AIDS in Uganda. He arrives in Uganda with his skeletal crew to inteview several authorities working at a center for the prevention of AIDS and to tape the everyday behavior of the local kids, including their singing and dancing. At night on the grounds of their luxury hotel, where the electricity is turned off at midnight, the crew converse in the darkness, reflecting on what they've seen. The next day, while a rainstorm is still in progress, they visit a nearby family taking care of several orphans in a semiruined house. An Austrian couple who have adopted a little girl who was found in the street becomes an important focus toward the end, and the film concludes with them leaving with the child for Vienna.

Sleepers (2001; video installation)
For a video installation presented at the Venice Biennale, Kiarostami taped a sleeping young couple and projected their life-size image for one hundred minutes onto an actual bed, with pillows and sheets, in an actual bedroom.

10 (*Ten;* 2002; feature)
Production: Abbas Kiarostami with Marin Karmitz (MK2 Productions)
Direction: Abbas Kiarostami
Screenplay: Abbas Kiarostami
Editing: Abbas Kiarostami with assistants Morteza Tabatabaii, Bahman Kiarostami, Mastaneh Mohajer, Vahid Ghazi Mirsoyid, Mazdak Sepanlu, Reza Yadzdani
Music: Howard Blake, "Walking in the Air"
Cast: Mania Akbari (driver), Amin Maher (her son, Amin), Roya Arabshahi, Katayoun Taleidzadeh, Mandana Sharbaf, Amene Moradi, and Kamran Adl
Other credited participants: Nazanin Joneydi, Christophe Rezai, Ali Boustan, Negar Raynani, Negin Rahimi, Noushien Agah, Mitra Farahani, and Nathalie Kreuther
Color

Digital video transferred to 35 mm
89 minutes
The film uses two digital video cameras mounted on the dashboard of a car to record the driver—a young, recently divorced, and remarried woman—and her passengers in ten sequences that are numbered in descending order. Her passengers include her son Amin, a female friend, her sister, a prostitute, and an old woman and a young woman who go to the same shrine. The sequences all begin with a number and the sound of a bell as at a sports event.

Note: Many film and video documentaries about Kiarostami have been made. Some of the most important of these are *Journey to the Land of the Traveler* (Bahman Kiarostami, 1993, 29 minutes), an encounter with Hasan Darabi, the actor who played the central character in *The Traveler; Abbas Kiarostami: Vérités et mensonges* (Jean-Pierre Limosin, 1994, 58 minutes, in the French television series *Cinéma de notre temps*); *Tarh* (Idea) (Bahman Kiarostami, 1997, 45 minutes), on the making of *Taste of Cherry; Kiarostami 101* (Jamsheed Akrami, 2000, 20 minutes); *Close-up Kiarostami* (Mahmoud Behraznia, 2000, 44 minutes); *Friendly Persuasion* (Jamsheed Akrami, 2001, 114 minutes); and *A Lesson in Cinema* (Majdeh Famili, 2002, 52 minutes) and *A Week with Kiarostami* (Yuji Mohara, 2002, 90 minutes) on the making of *The Wind Will Carry Us.*

Bibliography

Cheshire, Godfrey. "Confessions of a Sin-ephile: *Close-up*." *Cinema Scope*, no. 2 (Winter 2000): 3–8.

———. "How to Read Kiarostami." *Cineaste* 35.4 (2000): 9–10.

———. "The Short Films of Abbas Kiarostami." *Cinematexas* 5 (Oct. 16–22, 2000): 154–59.

Dabashi, Hamid. *Close Up: Iranian Cinema Past, Present, and Future*. New York: Verso, 2001.

Doraiswamy, Rashmi. "Abbas Kiarostami: Life and Much More." *Cinemaya: The Asian Film Quarterly* (Summer 1999): 18–20.

Ebert, Roger. *Roger Ebert's Movie Yearbook 2000*. Kansas City: Andrews McNeel Publishing, 2000.

Emami, Karim. "Recollections and Afterthoughts." <http://www.forughfarrokhzad.com>.

Farrokhzad, Forugh. *Bargozide-ye Ashar-e Forugh Farrokhzad* (A selection of the poems of Forugh Farrokhzad). 5th ed. Tehran: Sherkat-e Sahami-ye Ketabha-ye Jibi, 1977.

———. *Bride of Acacias: Selected Poems of Forugh Farrokhzad*. Trans. Jascha Kessler and Amin Banini. Delmar, N.Y.: Caravan Books, 1982.

———. *Remembering the Flight: Twenty Poems by Forugh Farrokhzad*. Bilingual ed. Trans. Ahmad Karimi-Hakkak. Port Coquitlam, Canada: Nik Publishers, 1997.

———. "The Wind Will Carry Us." Trans. David L. Martin. *Film Comment*, July–Aug. 2000, 25.

Ghoukasian, Zavin, ed. *Majmou-e-ye Maghalat dar Naghd-e va Moarrefi Asar-e Abbas Kiarostami* (A collection of articles criticizing and introducing the work of Abbas Kiarostami). Tehran: Nashr-e Didar, 1996.

Haghighat, Mamad, and Frédéric Sabouraud. *Histoire du cinéma Iranian, 1900–1999*. Paris: Centre Georges Pompidou/Bibliothèque Publique d'Information (Cinéma du Réel), 1999.

Hampton, Howard. "Lynch Mob." *Artforum* (Jan. 2000). <http://www.artforum.com>.

———. Responses to letters from Kent Jones and Jonathan Rosenbaum. *Artforum* (Mar. 2000). <http://www.artforum.com>.
Haydari, Gholam. *Forugh Farrokhzad Va Sinema* (Forugh Farrokhzad and cinema). Tehran: Nashr-e Elm, 1998.
Hedayat, Sadagh. *The Blind Owl*. Trans. D. P. Costello. New York: Grove Press, 1989.
———. *The Blind Owl and Other Hedayat Stories*. Comp. Carol L. Sayers. Ed. Russell P. Christensen. Minneapolis: Sorayya Publishers, 1984.
Hillmann, Michael C. *A Lonely Woman: Forugh Farrokhzad and Her Poetry*. Washington, D.C.: Three Continents Press/Mage Publishers, 1987.
Ishaghpour, Youssef. *Le réel, face, et pile: Le cinéma d'Abbas Kiarostami* (Reality, heads and tails: The films of Abbas Kiarostami). Tours: Farrago, 2000.
Islami, Majid, Houshang Golmakani, and Iran Karimi. "A Group Interview with Kiarostami: Goal: An Eliminating of Directing." *Film Monthly* (Tehran) 12.168: 121.
Jalal al-Din Rumi, Maulana. *A Garden beyond Paradise: The Mystical Poetry of Rumi*. Trans. Jonathan Star and Shahram Shiva. New York: Bantam Books, 1992.
———. *Kolliyat-e Shams* (Collected poems). Trans. Franklin D. Lewis. Ed. Badi Al-Zaman Faruzanfar. Tehran: Tehran University Press, 1967.
Jones, Kent. Letter to the editor. *Artforum* (Mar. 2000). <http://www.artforum.com>.
Kamshad, Hassan. *Modern Persian Prose Literature*. Bethesda, Md.: Iranbooks, 1996.
Karimi, Iraj. *Abbas Kiarostami, Filmsaz-e Realist* (Abbas Kiarostami: The realistic filmmaker). Tehran: Nashr-e Ahoo, 1987.
Kiarostami, Abbas. *Abbas Kiarostami: Textes, entretiens, filmographie complète*. Petite Bibliothèque des Cahiers du cinéma. Paris: Cahiers du cinéma, 1997.
———. "A Good, Good Citizen." Trans. Minou Moshiri. *Film International* 3.2 (Spring 1995): 54–61.
———. *Le goût de la cerise* (Cutting continuity of *Taste of Cherry*). *L'avant-scène cinéma*, no. 471 (Apr. 1998).
———. "Le monde d'A.K." *Cahiers du cinéma*, no. 493 (July–Aug. 1995).
———. "Love and the Wall." *Film International* 6.21 (Spring 1994): 61–65.
———. *Photographies, Photographs, Fotografie. . . .* Trilingual ed. Paris: Editions Hazan, 1999.
Makhmalbaf, Mohsen. "Makhmalbaf Film House." In *The Day I Became a Woman*. Trans. Babak Mozaffari. Bilingual ed. Tehran: Rowzaneh Kar, 2000. 5–9.
Marker, Chris. "Salgard-e Forugh Farrokhzad" (The anniversary of Forugh Farrokhzad). *Talash* 8 (Feb. 1967): 16.
Naficy, Hamid. *An Accented Cinema: Exilic and Diasporic Filmmaking*. Princeton: Princeton University Press, 2001.

Nancy, Jean-Luc, and Abbas Kiarostami. *L'Evidence du film.* Trilingual ed. Brussels: Yves Gevaert Editeur, 2001.
Omid, Jamal. *Tarikh-e Cinema-ye Iran* (History of Iranian cinema). Tehran: Entesharat-e Rozaneh, 1995.
Perez, Gilberto. "History Lessons." *The Material Ghost: Films and Their Medium.* Baltimore: Johns Hopkins University Press, 1998. 266–70.
Rosenbaum, Jonathan. "The Death of Hulot." *Placing Movies: The Practice of Film Criticism.* Berkeley: University of California Press, 1995. 163–79.
———. "From Iran with Love." *Chicago Reader,* Sept. 29, 1995.
———. "Iranian Sights." *Chicago Reader,* Oct. 23, 1992.
———. "Lessons from a Master." *Chicago Reader,* June 14, 1996, 45–47.
———. Letter to the editor. *Artforum* (Mar. 2000). <http://www.artforum.com>.
———. "Tati's Democracy." *Movies as Politics.* Berkeley: University of California Press, 1997. 37–40.
Saeed-Vafa, Mehrnaz. "Bresson, Naghash-i ke ba Cinemayash Sher Migouyad" (Bresson, a painter who writes poetry with his images). *Cinema Haft* 35 (May–July 1978): 5–21.
———. "Sohrab Shahid Saless: A Cinema of Exile." In *Life and Art: The New Iranian Cinema.* Ed. Rose Issa and Sheila Whitaker. London: National Film Theatre, 1999. 135–44.
Sepehry, Sohrab. *The Expanse of Green: Poems of Sohrab Sepehry.* Trans. David L. Martin. Los Angeles: Kalimet Press/UNESCO, 1988.
Shabani Pirposhteh, Mohammad, ed. *Tarhi Az Doust: Negahi be Zendegi va Asar-e Filmsaz-e Andishmand Abbas Kiarostami* (A profile of a friend: A look at the life and works of Abbas Kiarostami, a thoughtful filmmaker). Tehran: Entesharat-e Rozaneh, 1997.
Young, Deborah. Rev. of *10. Variety* (May 27–June 2, 2002): 2.

Index

Mehrnaz Saeed-Vafa is a filmmaker, a film teacher at Columbia College in Chicago, and the author of essays on Iranian cinema.

Jonathan Rosenbaum is the author of *Movie Wars, Movies as Politics, Greed, Dead Man,* and other books. He is a film critic for the *Chicago Reader.*

Books in the series Contemporary Film Directors

Nelson Pereira dos Santos
Darlene J. Sadlier

Abbas Kiarostami
Mehrnaz Saeed-Vafa and Jonathan Rosenbaum

The University of Illinois Press
is a founding member of the
Association of American University Presses.

Composed in 10/13 New Caledonia
with Helvetica Neue Extended display
by Jim Proefrock
at the University of Illinois Press
Designed by Paula Newcomb
Manufactured by Cushing-Malloy, Inc.

University of Illinois Press
1325 South Oak Street
Champaign, IL 61820-6903
www.press.uillinois.edu